MW00674710

LEARNING

TO LOVE GOD

Designed *for* Relationship

WITH

ALL WE ARE

T.J. MacLeslie

Parvaim Press
Seattle, Washington

Parvaim Press is committed to the practical expression of God's love in a world filled
with pain and suffering. All net profits benefit Kingdom-minded ministry around the world.
www.parvaimpress.com

Designed for Relationship: Learning to Love God with All We Are
© 2013 T.J. MacLeslie.

All rights reserved. Except for brief excerpts for ministry purposes, no part of this publication
may be produced in any form without written permission from Parvaim Press.

Scripture quotations are taken from the Holy Bible, New Living Translation,
copyright © 1996, 2004, 2007 by Tyndale House Foundation. Used by permission
of Tyndale House Publishers, Inc., Carol Stream, Illinois 60188. All rights reserved.

Cover and page design: Neil Angove Ltd. www.neilangove.ltd.uk
Cover photography: Neil Angove Ltd.

Names have been changed, as well as other potentially identifying details
to protect the privacy of the respective individuals.

ISBN 978-0-9890166-2-9 (Hardback)

THIS BOOK IS DEDICATED
TO THE COMMUNITY THAT IS GOD
AND TO THE COMMUNITY GOD HAS GIVEN ME
TO SHARE THE JOURNEY ON EARTH

ALSO BY T.J. MACLESLIE

PURSUIT OF A THIRSTY FOOL

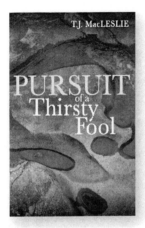

For more information, please visit
www.thirstyfool.com

Contents

CONTENTS

"*Designed for Relationship* is a lively and creative roadmap of insights written in a personal style revealing what it takes for you to develop a healthy and dynamic relationship with God. Filled with helpful cues and inventive insights, this book will guide any thirsty soul to a fresh discovery of the heart of God and the abundant life He has promised every believer."

DR. JERRY RUEB, *Lead Pastor,*
Cornerstone Church, Long Beach, California

"TJ MacLeslie brings wisdom and balance in what it means to experience relationship with God and live with Him in a more life-giving and full-orbed way. I believe this will be a great resource for leaders to whom I minister; not only for themselves but also for those they touch through ministry."

ELLEN BURANY, *Spiritual Director and Team Leader*
ChurchNEXT, Church Resource Ministries

"If the passion in your eyes has dimmed over the years, leaving you longing for a deeper draught of God, or if you disciple others and yearn to lead them in ways that open up richer intimacy with God, then this book will prove a blessing."

CLIFF POWELL, Ph.D., *Clinical Psychologist,*
The Mindspace, Sydney, Australia
Author of Unloading the Overload

"In medicine we have a tendency to treat only a patient's body and neglect other areas that can affect a person's health. In the Church, we often commit a similar error by applying the same spiritual remedies to all ailments. *Designed for Relationship* seeks to correct this error. I recommend this book for new Christians, for those who feel stagnant in their relationship with God, for Christian leaders that provide spiritual direction to others, and for anyone who is seeking to love God with their whole being."

DAN FLAMING, M.D.
Plano, Texas

"TJ McLeslie's *Designed for Relationship* offers hope to all who hunger and thirst for a deeper, more authentic intimacy with God. His 'Five Circles' concept, formed in the crucible of sometimes painful life experience and tested in the arena of Kingdom ministry, provides a holistic understanding of how God has designed us and offers practical help for taking intentional steps toward a rich and growing relationship with God. I have been spurred on to deeper intimacy with God through my friend's life, and I am confident that readers will be encouraged and inspired by his book."

ERIC PETERS, *International Director,*
Pioneers

Foreword

When I grew up in Michigan, we would look out the window and watch the first winter snowfall believing that this year we would win the snowman contest. If we calculated right and patiently waited for enough snow to fall, we knew there was the possibility of winning the contest, so we would wait. If built too soon, the snowballs would inevitably gather up dead leaves, sticks, and dirt, requiring us to patch the dirty parts of the snowman with clean white snow. If there was too much dirt and debris and not enough snow, the sun became a problem. Chunks of his body would melt or his eyes and mouth would slip or fall because of the debris and pretty soon the snowman was an unrecognizable mess.

Our lives are much like that of the snowman. We tend to quickly cover up the sin or what we don't like in our lives with knowledge, skill, pleasure, or scripture, making us look more resilient to crisis than we are. We tend to strive to make things look better and think we can clean our own selves up. We also tend not to believe that trials and suffering in our life can be used for good and make us more mature if we are willing to learn from them and grow through them. Instead we begin to believe we can maintain the good image we are presenting to the world that in reality is full of debris and ready to fall apart when something bumps it. No one is there to patch us up.

Today, many people are living out their own desires and do not know Jesus, others know him and are striving in their lives to work hard for Jesus. Relational concepts like intimacy, marriage, family, or community are no longer defined or understood and therefore have lost their meaning. Being controlled by desire, individual events in people's lives drive a part of their soul into some form of isolation. These events may be physical, mental, spiritual, the result of decisions, or life transitions. The result is the same, they are alone, unknown, and isolated from God and others.

In isolation, we cover what we don't like and hide from ourselves and others and we work harder to fill ourselves with what is pleasurable leading to a self-defeating addictive life style cut off from God and others.

Designed for Relationship, as the title expresses, is about how to live our lives walking with Jesus and others, for which we were created. In relationship we uncover by coming into the light and look for God's good for us rather than live for our own wants and desires. It is not easy to live as 'citizens of heaven' and as 'strangers and exiles on earth' as the writer of Hebrews says in Hebrews 13:13-16. Our cultural model for relationships is one of tolerance that accepts what is currently happening as normative and not making value judgments on what relationships should look like. Freedom for oneself and the personal right to choose is demanded without responsibility for anyone who might be hurt or affected.

God designed a very different way, unlike the other citizens of earth; we forgive sin readily, face the consequences of one another's sinfulness together, and humbly help each other cooperate with the Holy Spirit's work in us. Christ's death pays the price for our sin and sets us apart as truly different people. God's model, implanted in us at creation, is the Holy Trinity that teaches us about right relationship. The trinity is our pattern, equal, distinct, ordered, and unified in mutual love. This pattern reorders our relationships. In obedience we are to remain in the Father's love, and as we are pruned through the circumstances of life, the body of Christ holds us in His love.

As Professor of Spirituality and Marriage and Family at Talbot School of Theology it is a special gift for a former student to write a book in my unique area of passion. *Designed for Relationship* will help you move forward in your relationship with God and others so as to become more and more a reflection of God's design. This is fulfilling your purpose in becoming a fuller reflection of who God is to the world around you, and that will bring God glory.

JUDY TENELSHOF, Ph.D.
Professor of Spirituality and Marriage and Family

Director, Spiritual Formation Focus,
Institute for Spiritual Formation,
Talbot School of Theology/Biola University,
LaMirada, California

Founder: Hilltop Renewal Center

Preface

In more than 20 years of ministry, I have had the privilege of journeying alongside many people. God has moved me from place to place more than I would have liked. Along the way, I have met and ministered to some amazing people. I have lived on three continents and been involved in some incredible faith communities. I am sure I have received much more than I have given.

One of the important things I have learned along the way is the centrality of listening. In my early years, I tended to rush people through the machine of ministry – answering questions they weren't asking and offering solutions that didn't apply. I frequently offered 'solutions' drawn from personal lessons learned, conferences attended, or books read. I projected my own experience onto others and assured them that my advice was right.

Graciously, God has given me the experience of being stumped in ministry. I have run into many cases where my easy answers did not yield the results others hoped for. I've found myself in situations where just teaching the truth and calling people to obedience failed to produce the freedom, joy, and power that Jesus showed us in His life. Those frustrating experiences drove me back to God, and propelled my search for a better way.

This book contains many lessons I wish I'd learned earlier. Perhaps if someone had painted this picture for me, I'd have found the path to God more easily. I don't know. I do know that God encourages us to comfort others with the comfort we have received.[1] He calls us to share our lives and lessons and to spur one another on to love and good deeds.[2] This book is my attempt to do just that.

I do not present these insights as a finished work. I intend to be a lifelong learner, continuing to grow and change, both personally and in my ministry paradigm as well. I see this book as part of a larger conversation in the community of God-seekers that is the Church. I have written with the hope of helping people grapple with who they were created to be – it's my desire to spur them on toward God, and encourage them on their journey to become who they are.

T.J. MacLeslie

Tai'r Heol
Ystradfellte
Wales

Introduction

Have you ever been stuck?

As a teenager, some friends and I thought it would be cool to drive my Volkswagen 'Thing' along a deserted stretch of beach. It was fun at first, bouncing across the sand heading toward the water, but before long we were stuck. I revved the engine and popped the clutch to get us moving again, but the spinning wheels carved deepening holes in the loose sand. We tried everything we could think of to get the car free. We simply didn't have the experience or equipment to make it happen. What had seemed like a good idea, a fun adventure, became a painfully frustrating evening of fits and starts. We took turns digging and pushing while looking for scraps of wood or other beach debris to put under the tires to create some traction in the shifting sands. Occasionally, we freed the car and made a few yards of progress only to become bogged down again. Our experience was nothing like the original vision. We cursed our foolishness and decided to never do that again.

I have met many people who would describe their Christian life in similar terms. They bought into a vision of Christianity that looked great on the brochure, but the reality turned out to be much more difficult and much less fun than they bargained for. Their

journey started well; however, they soon found themselves stuck
and ill-equipped to find a way out. No matter what they tried,
they could not gain traction to move forward on the journey. They
occasionally tasted freedom and joy only to become bogged down
again and again – the eternal kind of life more elusive than they
once imagined.

Jesus said that He came to give us abundant life.[3] For many
of us this vision remains tantalizingly out of reach. When we 'got
saved,' we may have experienced love, joy, and peace welling up
within us in ways we couldn't have imagined. Then, after attending
church and doing all the 'Christian stuff' for a while, the experience
seemed to fade. At this stage, many people lose hope and conclude
that either Christianity is not true or there is something wrong with
them – something that disqualifies them from the grace and love of
God. Nothing could be further from the truth.

So, why does this happen? Why does this experience of the
vibrant life fade? There is no single answer. Each person's life and
experience is unique. This is not a book with easy answers. I don't
have 'three keys to this' or 'seven steps to that.' Instead, I share the
lessons I have learned on my own journey. Along the way, I have
found a perspective of God and humanity that provides a framework
for understanding our personal experience. Rather than prescribing
a 'one size fits all' version of Christian spirituality, I am presenting
a context within which we can cultivate our own relationship with
God the Father, the Son, and the Holy Spirit in community with
each other. I have found that this relational approach to God and
life makes all the difference!

In my last book, *Pursuit of a Thirsty Fool*, I shared my story in
some detail. I am a thirsty fool. Over the years, I came to realize that
what I thirst for is God; I am not hungry for knowledge about God
or a philosophy of life that I can embrace, or a source of wisdom or
guidance. I am thirsty for God Himself.

Even after I finally surrendered to His love and entered into a committed relationship with Him, I continued to wander. I continued to drink from other cisterns, to pursue other lovers.[4] Like Gomer, God bought me back from my adulterous slavery again and again.[5] He declared His undying love for me and welcomed me in. No matter how many times I strayed, He loved me and welcomed me home.

The journey of intimacy does not end with the wedding. Marriage is another beginning, a pathway to new levels of intimacy. I have been married more than 17 years and our relationship continues to develop. I know my wife and am known by her much more deeply than when we started down this path. I have changed and matured along the way. Our ability to communicate has increased, our trust has deepened, and we have grown toward each other.

My relationship with God is very like a marriage. God established this relationship on the day I finally accepted His proposal. Having committed myself to Him, I renounced all others. Even though my record has not been one of perfect faithfulness, God is the perfect lover and spouse. He never forgets or gets distracted. He is always attentive and engaged. He is always ready to serve or to talk. He knows me better than I know myself, and He believes that I am capable of more than I know. He invites me to know Him and to walk with Him day by day.

God invites us into a real relationship with Him.[6] This has always been the invitation. He created us with the capacity for relationship. We are, at our core, relational beings. We routinely exercise this multifaceted relational capacity with one another, yet this capacity finds its highest expression in our relationship with God. Can you imagine the immensity of this concept? We can connect and communicate with the Creator of the Universe! We can actually know God as we know one another. We can talk to Him, and we can learn to hear His voice.

It takes time, energy, and intentionality to develop any relationship. We have to fight for intimacy. My relationship with my wife does not automatically grow. I am no saint and neither is she.[7] We are committed to each other and we choose day by day to nurture our relationship. When we make mistakes, we talk with each other, seek and give forgiveness, and move on. The same is true in my relationship with my kids, my parents, my siblings, or any other important relationship – even, and especially, my relationship with God.

Most of us are defeated before we even start the battle. We're beaten by our low expectations – a form of self-fulfilling prophecy. We do not believe we can actually have a committed, faithful, loving relationship with someone...and so we don't. We don't believe that we are lovable, so we wall ourselves off from whatever love might come our way. As a result, our relationships rarely exceed our expectations. We must find a way to hope and believe that more is possible before we will reach out for it.

In my last book, I shared the story of how God rekindled my hope and how He met and exceeded my expectations. I issued an invitation to hope. I firmly believe that if a foolish man like I can meet God and begin to hear His voice and live life in light of Him, anyone can.

I spend a lot of my time these days helping people on their journey, as they seek to pursue the Pursuer. I want to share with you what I share with them. I pray that you will be encouraged and will discover more about Him and about yourself in the pages that follow.

This book is divided into two parts:

Part One presents a renewed vision of God and our relationship with Him, inviting us to experience more of Him and pointing out obstacles we may face on the way. It begins with a parable to renew our vision that leads to a reexamination of the Gospel. This is followed by a pointed look at the centrality of our relationship with God. We then consider our response to God and explore how that response flows into our relationships with others. Part One concludes with an investigation of who we are as creatures made in God's image, including the introduction of a unique ministry paradigm – *The Five Circles*.

Part Two delves more deeply into each of *The Five Circles*: the core aspects of our humanity. Each chapter examines a specific aspect of our humanity through the lens of Scripture and connects it to our relationship with God. These chapters also contain real case studies to help us explore aspects of ourselves that we might not have considered, as well as practical suggestions for growth.

If you feel stuck, this book is for you. Perhaps your wheels are spinning and you just can't find the way forward. I can't promise that you will be whole, healed, and utterly free at the end of your reading; but I can tell you that I, and many others, have found wholeness, healing, and freedom walking with God on the paths outlined here.

Many of us are stuck but don't realize or feel it. Perhaps you are among those who have settled for less than all God offers you, like the child C.S. Lewis describes as content to play in a muddy slum because he cannot conceive of the beauty and joy of a trip to the beach.[8] This book is also for you. Many Christians live lives of quiet desperation, afraid to voice their questions because they are convinced they should have all the answers. I lived like that for a long time. As I began to voice my questions, I found many others who were thirsting for the eternal kind of life but felt alone, their hope slipping away. There are more of us than you think, and there is good reason to hope!

This book is also intended to serve as an aid for fellow pastors, ministry leaders, and spiritual directors. I know the burden of caring for others. Some people seem to need little help or encouragement; they appear to sail along in their journey toward God. Nevertheless, there are many in our flocks who need more. The path of these wounded people may tread ground we have never walked. Perhaps you are a person who bears some shepherding responsibility for others, but who finds the answers you know ineffective in helping the people you love. My hope is that this book will better equip you to care for your people and point them to Jesus along paths where they will find healing and freedom.

I pray that you will be encouraged by what you find here. I pray you will be propelled forward on your journey, no longer stuck in the sand or settling for less. May you be encouraged to intentionally cultivate your relationship with God, and find some fresh ideas about how to do so.

God is always previous. He is the One drawing us to Himself, wooing us with His love. Before we wanted Him, He wanted us. He created each of us on purpose for relationship with Him. The breakdown in our relationship with Him is not on His end. We need a renewed vision of God and of ourselves to encourage us forward into all He has intended.

Introduction: reflection questions

- *When have you felt stuck in your life?*
  In your relationship with God?

- *How have you experienced frustration or*
  disappointment in your walk with God?

- *How would you describe your eagerness to grow? Have you wrestled*
  with the challenge of whether real growth and life change is possible?

- *In what ways do you identify with those who*
  have lost hope for intimacy with God?

- *Why are you reading this book? How do you hope it will benefit you*
  as well as those you might desire to help along in their journey?

- *How much are you willing to invest in your relationship with God?*

PART ONE

Renewing Our Vision

Renewed Vision from an Old Story

There once was a man with two sons. This father loved his sons very much – more than they could comprehend. He expressed his love in many ways. He was generous and kind. He also loved them enough to correct them and was quite firm when necessary.

As the boys grew toward manhood, they began to draw away from him. Their father became concerned. He knew they needed some independence. They would need to become their own men; but he sensed in them something other than a healthy differentiation from himself. He sensed a growing resentment, even rebelliousness.

He was a patient father, so he continued to lavish his love on his boys and reach out to them. Each morning over breakfast, he would try to engage them in conversation. He shared his heart and experience of life and invited them to do the same. He remembered the times in their childhood when they would climb up on his lap and share their hurts, fears, or concerns…but no longer. His longing for dialogue was met with stony silence. Each expression of love was rejected, and the distance between them continued to grow.

Another source of concern was the course their sibling relationship was taking. They were increasingly distant from one another. He reminded them of their love for each other and often over dinner regaled them with stories from their childhood. These stories had always brought them together. Now, even these reminders of their shared life no longer had the power to unite. Where once there had been trust and laughter, now there were only smirks and antagonistic scowls.

Then one morning, it happened. The lurking shadow broke the surface, rearing its ugly head. His younger son could no longer contain his roiling emotions. He cursed his father

"You doddering old fool! Why do you keep on telling the old stories? Nobody cares about them! Nobody cares about you! Can't you see that we're just waiting around for you to die? I wish you were dead now and then I could have what is rightfully mine!" He screamed at his father, slamming his fist down on the table.

His hoarse voice choked with emotion, he continued, "Every day I see all this wealth around me, just out of reach. I'm tired of living like a kid with his face pressed up against the glass. I can see the sweets on the other side, but they are always just beyond my grasp. You say you love me…well prove it! Give me what is mine. Give me my inheritance now. I don't want to live on your supposedly benevolent generosity. I'm sick of coming to you, hat in hand; I'm tired of being your puppet on a string! I want my independence now! I want what is coming to me NOW! Give it to me and let me live my own life!"

When his screeching monologue was over, his father bowed his head. Tears welled up in his eyes and in a choking voice, he simply said, "Fine."

The seething son was stunned. At first, he thought he had misheard. All these years of pent up frustration couldn't be over this quickly, could they? "I don't believe you! I want the money, and I want it now!" he shouted.

"If that is what you want, then you shall have it. I will get everything prepared for you, and you can leave tomorrow morning," his father slowly replied. "You won't find what you're looking for this way, but…"

"NO! No more of your words! I'm sick of your pseudo-wisdom! Just have everything ready for me in the morning. That's all I want from you!" With that, the younger son stood up abruptly, knocking over his chair, and stormed out of the room.

The elder son sat quietly in his place. His father turned to him and asked, "What about you? What do you want my son? What can I do for you?"

"Nothing, father."

"Nothing? There is no way I can show you my love?"

"No father, I'm fine," he replied as he quietly resumed eating.

His father bowed his head again and a single tear streaked down his cheek.

After another silent ending to another painful meal, the father got up from the table to prepare for the departure of his son. There were a number of things to do in order to split his estate and give his son what he had asked for.

By the following morning, all was done. The disbelieving boy seized his inheritance and counted it. He had to be sure his father wasn't cheating him. That done, with a self-satisfied grin he turned to leave without as much as a thank you. His father reached out his hand as if to grasp his shoulder and turn his boy around for one last embrace, but his son violently shook him off and stalked out of the house. His father silently followed him out the front door and stood watching as his son walked out of his life.

His exhilarated son launched into a lavish lifestyle, the kind of life he had always known wealth would bring. He gathered an entourage. It wasn't difficult to find new friends as he splashed money around. He was generous and they enjoyed all that riches could provide. It was literally a dream come true for him. Every once in a while, the liberated young man would wake up with a pang of conscience, wondering about his father; but it never lasted long. He was always able to distract himself with another diversion, another experience, another party, another drink, another…another.

Every morning his grieving father woke up wondering about his son. Rather than distract himself, he would go and sit on the front porch. He would look up the road where his eyes had last rested on the vanishing figure of his son, and he would feel the weight of it again. He let himself feel the longing and love well up within him, and he turned all this into prayer.

Sometimes his older son would interrupt him and ask what he could do for him. His father usually responded with an invitation to come sit for a while; but the son always turned away at this. He wanted to *do* something…to *accomplish* something. Sitting in mourning for his idiot brother was not on the list.

The older son devoted himself to the family business. He was good; he was *very* good. He was a shrewd businessman and quick to spot an opportunity. After some time, the estate had more than doubled in value. That would show his brother! That would show his father!

He worked hard, late into the night. He rarely had dinner with the old man anymore, but he was sure his father understood. He was certain his father recognized that he was doing it all for him. He believed his father would come to see that he was the good, smart, loyal son – the one who deserved his father's love – and that he would forget about his reprobate little brother wasting his life and squandering his inheritance.

While the family estate grew and flourished, in the distance the younger son's demanded inheritance dwindled. At first it just meant that the parties were less frequent and the gifts less lavish. But as his withering wallet further pinched his generosity, he noticed his friends came around less often…some even disappearing altogether. One morning he woke up to the realization that he didn't have any money left…not even enough for food. "How has it come to this?" he wondered. He spent each day wandering around the city, looking for food and work, and finding neither. As darkness fell, he picked through the garbage looking for half-eaten scraps. He found enough to fill his belly and desperately hoped he wouldn't get sick. He also hoped there would be no trouble at night as he lay in an alley trying to sleep – a huddled, frightened bundle in the dark.

One morning as he awoke, his thoughts drifted back to his father and he wondered how the old man was. He remembered the meals at his father's table and longed to be there. He knew he had burned that bridge. There was no way back. He knew that.

But maybe…maybe he could get a job with the family business. He wouldn't expect to be welcomed at the house, but maybe his father would be willing to hire him. He would be different this time. He would work hard, like his brother. He got up, and dusted himself off – not that it helped much. His fine clothes were deeply stained and torn. He hadn't bathed in weeks, his hair was matted, and he smelled as bad as he felt. Even so, he got up and started for home, hoping there was still a chance for him.

His father sat lonely on the porch. It was raining that morning as he sat staring down the road like he did every morning, praying for his sons. What was that? He caught a movement out of the corner of his eye. Someone was coming. Who could that be? It looks like… no, it couldn't be…is it? Before he knew it, he was up out of his chair, starting down the front steps. Could it really be him?

He picked up speed as his hope propelled him down the walk and into the street. He couldn't move very quickly at his age, but his excitement overwhelmed his caution. He saw the possibility that this could be his son; soon he was running toward him. Whoever it was, he was moving slowly, as if each step was torturously painful. He was close enough, but couldn't see his face…if only the man would look up he would know for sure. "Oh please, please let it be my son!" As the prayer escaped the father's lips, the sound surprised the approaching man; he looked up to see an old man running toward him. The flash of recognition struck them both at the same time. The father threw open his arms and the son dropped to his knees.

"Please father! Don't touch me. I'm too dirty for your embrace. I'm not worthy of your love. I don't come expecting you to love me or take me back. I know I was wrong. I just need some food and a job. Please can you just give me a job?" The words tumbled out as he fixed his eyes on the ground.

His father didn't hear what the young man said, or if he did, he didn't care. He threw himself on his son and embraced him with a fierceness and strength that belied his years. He was weeping. He kept saying over and over again, "My boy has come home! My boy has come home!" Soon the son was weeping too. He didn't know what was going to happen next but it felt good to experience his father's love again. He wasn't thinking about food or work now. He let his fear melt away as he shared an embrace with his dad.

After a few minutes, his father regained some of his composure and pulled his son to his feet. "Come with me, my son. We will get you cleaned up." He took off his robe and draped it over his son's shoulders as he turned to lead him back to the house. They must have looked quite a sight, the old man in his pajamas leading the shaggy homeless person into his home. Neither of them cared.

The son showered and shaved, and found his father had laid out fresh clothes for him. After he was cleaned up, they had breakfast. The son was so overwhelmed he didn't know what to say. His father just smiled at him from across the table. Finally, his father broke the silence, "I wondered if this day would ever come." As the son braced himself for the anticipated rebuke, his father continued. "Welcome home my son. I have missed you so much. It must have been terrible for you out there. Now you have come home to me." His words were so kind and gentle, and his smile so genuine. It dawned on his son that no rebuke was coming. He could hardly believe it. He wondered how well he really knew his father.

"Now about the business of being worthy of my love…" his father continued, "we'll have no more talk about that. It has never been about you being worthy. You are my son and I love you. I have always loved you. No matter where you go, what you do, or who you become, I will always love you. I will always be your father and you will always be my beloved son. Nothing can change that. Let's get to know each other again. It will take time, and it may be difficult, but it will be worth the effort. I want to share my life with you and to be a part of yours as well. I don't want to give you a job. My hope is that you will enter into my love. I want us to begin working together as father and son. Would that be okay with you?"

"Of course…it's just…I don't know what else to say…I'm so sorry…Please forgive me…I…I…" He stammered to a stop. There was so much he wanted to say, but where to start…how to express… words failed him.

"I know you are. I love you and I forgive you. I am eager for us to move on, but happy to hear whatever you want to tell me, whenever you are ready. For now, just know that I love you, and…" he paused with a twinkle in his eye.

"And what, father?"

"And I am going to throw you a party tonight! A welcome home party!"

"I'm not sure I'm up for it dad. Won't you be embarrassed? I'm ashamed of myself, of what I've done."

"Ahhhh, I see," said his father, frowning, "But the thing is…I'm not ashamed of you!" He broke into a wide smile as he continued, "I'm not embarrassed. I'm excited that my son has come home. No one else need know anything but the joy of our reunion! Tonight we will share our happiness with those who will rejoice with us. You are happy to be back aren't you?"

"Yes, of course; but my head's still spinning a bit. I woke up this morning in the gutter and tonight I'll be the guest of honor in the house of my father."

"No, tonight you'll be the guest of honor in *our* house – not mine, but ours! It has always been ours. Tonight we enter into a new phase of our relationship, a new life together. You were lost to me long before you left this house, but you have come home. Now our relationship is restored and if that's not worthy of a party, I don't know what is!" His father was beaming and his happiness was infectious. How could he argue with that? And why bother trying? He decided to rest in his father's love.

His father planned an extravagant party. It was more lavish and fun than any party he had thrown during his time away. There was something different, something genuine and free about the whole atmosphere. No one was trying to gain an advantage over or use another. He had never been to a party like this and he really liked it...until his older brother showed up.

The front door flew open and his brother stood in the doorway with fire in his eyes and a scowl on his face. There was a party and no one had invited him. What in the world was going on here? Then his eyes found his idiot brother's face in the crowd. His jaw slowly dropped open, his face hardened and he made a beeline for his father, grabbing him by the arm and spinning him roughly out of the room.

His face, twisted with rage, was only inches from his father's as he hissed, "What is going on here?" Without pausing for a response he launched into his tirade, "What's HE doing here? I've been slaving away for you all these years, trying to make up for what he stole from you and you've never thrown me a party. You have never appreciated all I've done for you. But HIM! He wished you were dead! He left and never even sent word! I've been here all these years working hard for you and this is the way you repay me! You throw a party for that worthless piece of..."

"Hold on!" his father interrupted him. "Everything I have is yours. You know that. You have been with me all these years, and I am always here for you. Your brother was lost. He was gone all this time. He could have died out there; but now he's back and I am making things new again. Come into the party! Share in our joy!"

Jesus was a master storyteller. I hope I have done justice to His story in this retelling.[9] One of the things I love about His stories is their richness; they are so full of meaning. They don't lay all the diamonds right on the surface – sometimes you have to dig for them. His stories can sneak up and surprise you. Even when you are familiar with them, they can suddenly slip past your defenses and zing you.

I love this story about the father and two sons. It is commonly called the story of the *Prodigal Son*, but that label causes us to miss things and pre-programs us to read the story from a particular perspective. The story is really about the father and both of the sons. If we think of it as the story of the *prodigal son*, we can miss the nuances. We can fail to notice what is happening with the father or with the other son.

It is natural to focus on the shockingly bad son. His departure and the squandering of his inheritance are dramatic moments in the story. Jesus draws us in with the drama and we don't anticipate the ending. Then, Jesus leaves us hanging. He doesn't tie up the story with a nice bow and an epilogue. He leaves us standing outside the party with the tension hanging in the air between the father and the son who never physically left.

I don't know how many times I have read this story. I can't begin to count all of the times that I've heard it, or variations of it, over the course of my life. Recently, God has drawn my attention back to the story again. As I've reflected on it, I've caught something new: The two brothers make essentially the same mistake – they both leave their father. They take different paths, but they are both prodigals in their own way because they are both focused on the riches. The younger son is the wild child. He chooses the socially unacceptable form of outright rebellion and desertion. Yet the older son is also missing what the father has to offer. He has been physically with his father all along, but has deserted him just the same.

The older son's main gripe when his father throws the party for his brother is that he has been slaving away and never received even a young goat for a party with his friends.[10] Notice that he wants to have a party *with his friends*, not a party *with his father*. Just like his brother, he is yearning for independence. The difference is that whereas his younger brother takes the money and runs, the eldest stays around and works hard. His work has nothing to do with love for his father; rather, it's all about taking his father's stuff and having a party *of his own*.

He is similar to the misguided Christians James describes: "You are jealous of what others have, but you can't get it, so you fight and wage war to take it away from them. Yet you don't have what you want because you don't ask God for it. And even when you ask, you don't get it because your motives are all wrong – you want only what will give you pleasure."[11] The older brother wants something *from* the father, but he doesn't really want the *father*.

The real tragedy of the story is that the father has been available to both of his sons throughout the entire story, but neither one wanted what he offered. What is he offering? He is offering *himself*. He is offering *relationship*.

In the last few years, God has been opening my eyes to see what was there all along: relationship is at the core of everything. And when I say everything, I really mean *everything*. From the very first chapter of the Bible to the very last, it is all about relationship.

Before man was even created, there was relationship. In the first chapter of the Bible, we find God having a conversation with Himself. The mysterious Three-in-One God decides to make human beings in Their image. The plural pronouns are right there in the text. He says, "Let us make…in our image, to be like us."[12] Before any humans existed, God was already in an eternally existent community with Himself, or Themselves.

The Trinity is an often-neglected core truth about God. I have some trepidation in approaching the topic at all. It is, after all, a paradox and a profound mystery, beyond my ability to comprehend fully. However, it is true and important. I cannot fully explain the Trinity, but I can highlight its significance as I experience His presence. The Trinitarian nature of God means that God is inherently community, inherently relational.

The purpose of this book is not to espouse or defend particular theological positions; however, one cannot write about God with any degree of clarity without taking a particular position. This book is not about defending the doctrine of the Trinity; rather, it is a call to re-engage and re-experience God as He is in His Trinitarian nature.

I struggle with how to describe the Trinity. It's not that I struggle with the reality of the Trinity; I struggle with the confines of language when trying to express it.[13] There is only One God. That is true and explicitly taught, but this One God expresses Himself as three distinct persons. When do we use singular pronouns and when do we use plural ones? When I say "God," I mean the "Community of Divine Persons that is the Godhead." Yet I wonder what other people hear when I say that? If I refer to God as Them, does that make me sound polytheistic? God uses plural pronouns to describe Himself. My use of unfamiliar pronouns is not intended to shock or cause discomfort, but rather to spur us to think carefully about what we really mean when we are talking about God.

God exists as a Them as much as a Him. God the Father, God the Son, and God the Holy Spirit are all equally God. This is no small thing. This Trinitarian understanding of God is right at the core of life, the universe, and everything. God is interdependent within Himself. He exists, and has always existed in relationship. The created order expresses this interdependence. Even before the creation of man, interdependence and diversity permeated creation. When God created humankind in Their image, He created them male and female. He created relational, communal, interdependent beings with the power to relate to one another and to Himself. He blessed them and encouraged them to continue to create community and live in right relationship with the Godhead, with one another, and with the whole created order.[14] This ability to choose relationship is one mark of His image in us. He made us to live connected to Him. We are most human, we are most alive, and we are most ourselves when in union with Him. As our relationship with God develops, we will grow in all facets of ourselves. As we grow in unity with God and harmony with ourselves, we move toward right relationship with all other elements of God's creation.

This theme of relationship fills the Scriptures. In the very last chapter of the Bible, John tells us that Jesus is coming again. Jesus Himself said He is coming soon.[15] How does that strike you? Can you see Him running down the street toward you with open arms? John enthusiastically responds to Jesus, saying, "Come!"[16] He is clearly excited about Jesus' return. In fact, he says we don't have to wait until Jesus comes again to experience Him. John tells us, "Let anyone who is thirsty come. Let anyone who desires drink freely from the water of life."[17] John is clearly recalling Jesus' invitation to come to Him, and the promise He made that the Spirit would spring up within us if we do.[18]

From the first chapter to the very last, the pages of Scripture are an invitation to, and an expression of, relationship. This relational orientation brings the Scriptures to life. In fact, if we don't have this relational view we are missing the point of Scripture. Listen to Jesus' rebuke of the Pharisees: "You search the Scriptures because you think they give you eternal life. But the Scriptures point to me! Yet you refuse to come to me to receive this life."[19]

Jesus came that we might have life – abundant, full life.[20] He modeled for us the kind of life that is available to us. He said that we would do even more amazing things than He did.[21] He told us that real life is to know God the Father and Jesus Christ.[22] He taught us that He is the life, and that there is no other way to get to know the Father except through Him.[23]

Repeatedly throughout the pages of Scripture God expresses His heart for us and His invitation to life with Him. He also shows us what happens when we choose life apart from Him. He loves us too much not to tell us the whole story, just as I love my children too much not to warn them of the consequences of touching a hot stove.

All too often, we are like the sons in the story. We want what we can get from God, and we want it on our terms. We miss the best thing God is offering us. He withholds no good gift from His children, and He wants to give us the best Gift. He wants to give us Himself.

Jesus uses the example of fatherhood again in Luke 11, where He says this, "You fathers – if your children ask for a fish, do you give them a snake instead? Or if they ask for an egg, do you give them a scorpion? Of course not! So if you sinful people know how to give good gifts to your children, how much more will your heavenly Father give the Holy Spirit to those who ask him."[24]

Notice that what the Father offers to give us is Himself. Our Father will not withhold anything good from us, *and* He will give the Holy Spirit to us. This truth comes at the end of a short teaching on prayer. Jesus doesn't teach us a prayer methodology we can use to compel God to give us the stuff we want. He concludes His sermon on prayer by assuring us that God is an even better father than we can imagine, and that God loves to give Himself to us![25]

As I have continued to reflect on the story of the prodigal *sons*, another more subtle problem comes to light. It's not just that the sons misunderstand their father; they also fail to see themselves as the father sees them. They think either too highly or too lowly of themselves. They fail to trust the father and they fail to see themselves as they really are. How often are we like one of the two sons? How often have we reduced God to a sort of cosmic vending machine where we think we can demand stuff from him (like the younger son) or earn stuff from him (like the older son)? How often do we see ourselves as unlovable, or fall into pride in our performance? Both perspectives keep us from experiencing all God has to offer. The great present is before us. Will we unwrap it, or leave it unopened and untouched?

Will we come to the party?

Chapter 1: reflection questions

- *Whom do you identify with in the story?
  The younger son, older son, or the father?*

- *In what ways are you seeking satisfaction
  for your soul apart from God?*

- *What false ideas about God might be holding you
  back from experiencing all God has for you?*

- *What wrong ideas do you believe about yourself that
  might be inhibiting your intimacy with God?*

- *How does the Trinity shape your understanding of
  God and your relationship with Him / Them?*

- *How are you responding to God's invitation to
  come to the party and share in His joy?*

Re-examining the Good News

This relational understanding of God and humanity is perhaps the central truth around which all other truth revolves. We are inherently relational beings, and this is an important aspect of the image of God in us. God is a relational community. It is impossible to talk about the Triune God without implicitly acknowledging the relationship at the center of the Godhead. God is Three and One. These three personalities are now and have always been in relationship with one another. He created us in Their image.

We were created with the capacity to relate to Them and we did so initially. But then we failed on our end of the relationship by believing a lie and choosing to disobey.[26] This first sin ruptured the relationship. It marred the image of God in us and nearly destroyed the world. Today we live in a damaged world that mirrors the harm we have done to our relationship with God.

The image of God in us was not completely destroyed, but our intimate relationship with God was ruined. Our ability to perceive Him was not entirely lost, but our personal connection was obliterated. One of the ways that anyone may still perceive God is through nature.[27] We can observe His handiwork and learn about His character in His creation; but our ability to walk and talk with Him and partner with Him in the family business was lost. Our dead relationship needed resurrecting, and only God could do it. So He did.

We could not reach Him, so He reached out to us. In the Gospel of John, we are told the Word became flesh.[28] The Word, the Idea behind all ideas, emptied Himself of His divine power and humbled Himself.[29] One of the three eternally existent personalities that make up the Godhead took on human flesh and lived a human life. This is a profound mystery. How is it that God could lay aside some of His attributes and be born a human? Yet this mystery makes the possibility of an authentic relationship with God a reality. God understands humanity because He walked a mile in our shoes... from the cradle to the Cross. He bridged the divide between us and Them. His commitment to broaden the circle of relationship beyond the Trinity – to invite us back into this eternally vibrant life, to make us partakers of the divine nature – went to this unthinkable extent.[30]

We were created for a relationship with God. All too often we settle for something less. The story of Scripture, from beginning to end, is not one of great saints who have pursued God, but of a great God who pursues sinners. This is good news. Somehow, we have lost sight of it.

I have been living in Wales for the last couple of years.[31] While it has been a delight to live where I regularly hear church bells rather than the Islamic call to prayer, I've also found that my expectations that I was moving into a specifically Christian context in Wales have not been fulfilled. Wales, and I suppose much of Europe, is quickly becoming post-Christian. There are true followers of Christ here, but they are rare. Having previously lived in an overwhelmingly Muslim context where there was little or no knowledge about Christ, we found that the general lack of information has created cautious interest in Christianity. In contrast, most people we live among now are familiar with the basic facts of the Christian message, but have little interest in God, cautious or otherwise. They are familiar with the words, and even repeat them when culturally called upon to do so, yet they pay no attention to the meaning. The words have lost their power. Familiarity has bred apathy.

Part of the problem is this: the version of Christianity that they have been exposed to bears little resemblance to the actual message of Christ. Christianity has been presented as a sort of self-improvement philosophy, a mere list of 'dos' and 'don'ts', or perhaps a comforting cosmology that helps to define our place in the universe. Unbelievers did not perpetrate this twisting of the message. We believers did this. Christians have reduced the Gospel to much less than God intends. We have become modern-day Pharisees who tithe and attend church, while failing to love God or people.[32] G.K. Chesterton said it this way, "The Christian ideal has not been tried and found wanting, it has been found difficult and left untried."[33] In our hesitancy to fully embrace the Gospel lifestyle, we have given people the wrong impression about who God is, who we are as His children, and what He invites us to.

The truth is that God can be known; He has revealed Himself. We can have an actual relationship with God. This statement may not sound astounding to you, but it is! The staggering message of salvation is no longer staggering to us, because it has lost its shock value. It's not that it's no longer *good* news; it's just *yesterday's* news to many Christians. Many of us have heard this message so many times that we have been inoculated against the power of it.

This was not always the case. There was a time when we first heard the message. We had been living in ignorance of the good news that the God of heaven and earth came down and lived as a man. This God-man died to destroy death and was resurrected to restore life. The Almighty God whom humankind had offended and spurned made a way to restore us to fullness of life and to restore our relationship with Him. This is actually good news – shockingly, amazingly, great news! Nevertheless, to those of us who grew up hearing it a couple of times each week, it may seem commonplace. We often fail to marvel at the wonder of the Gospel.

Yet this marvelous news is still unknown to many. They don't know what is available to them. Millions of people have never even heard the invitation to a real relationship with God. I have had the privilege of carrying this startlingly good news to people for the first time. I have seen suspicion give way to surprise, then amazement give way to hope, and finally hope erupt into joy as they have tasted and seen that God really exists and that He rewards those who diligently seek Him.[34]

Christianity is the only major world religion (although I hesitate to call it a religion, as it is so much more) that promises an intimate relationship with God.[35] We are the only ones with this good news, but it does not belong to us. We did not create it. We must not keep this good news to ourselves. The Devil has concocted lies to keep people from hoping or to cause them to seek satisfaction in something other – something less.

The lies are diverse and complex, but the truth is ridiculously simple. God is. God loves. God saves. We were made for Him. We are designed to live in relationship with Him. We have rebelled against Him and rejected Him, but He was not satisfied to leave us to our own devices.[36] He has broken into the story.[37] The definitive act of salvation has already taken place. We are living in the denouement of history. The victory has been won – all that remains is the working out of it. He is making all things new![38] The table has been set, the invitations have been printed – and all that remains is to deliver them before the banquet begins.[39]

However, if the good news no longer seems good to us, why would we invite people to join us in our unhappiness? If we have exchanged the glory of an interactive relationship with God for mere performance of religious duty or attempted moral superiority then it is no longer good news. We are invited to taste and see that the Lord is good, but we reject this invitation.[40] Instead, we act like the Israelites during the Exodus, who cried out to Moses, "You speak to us, and we will listen. But don't let God speak directly to us, or we will die!"[41] We act as if God is a tyrant, bent on our destruction, rather than a community of love inviting us to enter.

God goes to great lengths to reveal Himself to us.[42] He reveals Himself through creation in myriad ways – from the awesome power of the sun to the gentle doe caring for her fawn. He reveals Himself in His interactions with humankind, recorded in the Scriptures. He reveals Himself through His personal interactions with us even now. He is transcendent and mysterious, and yet very present. He is closer to us than our own breath and is eager to be discovered.

From Abraham to Moses, Augustine to Patrick, David Brainerd to Frank Laubach, stories of personal encounters with God infuse Scripture and history. The stories of Abraham's and Moses' experiences are recorded in Scripture, as well as the experiences of hundreds of other biblical figures. But personal encounters with God did not only occur in the biblical era. History records many stories of people personally meeting God in the course of their lives right up to today. The stories of Augustine, the 4th-century church leader and writer, and Patrick, the famous missionary to Ireland, have encouraged people for generations. The stories of Brainerd, an 18th-century missionary in North America, and Laubach, A 20th-century missionary to the Philippines, are more recent additions to this long list of pilgrims.[43] These six, are only a smattering of the many whose interactions with God have been captured and made available for those of us who would follow their example. The interactive nature of God is scattered throughout the pages of history. It has always been there. I sit here shaking my head in wonder as to how I missed it for so many years.

As we relate to Him as He really is, we will increasingly understand who we really are. When we put our relationship with God back in the center of the story, we regain an accurate perspective of ourselves as well. We will know that God is for us and stop reading Scripture through the lens of our shallow desires.

The Bible is more than a manual for how to run your business or have a happy marriage. It is more than a gold-mine of principles that you can apply for your parenting or your social life. It is more than a prophetic rebuke of our cultural and racial prejudices. It is ultimately the story of God's interactions with particular people and with humankind as a whole. It is the story of a broken family being restored. We are all part of that family, playing different roles in the revelation of redemption.

CHAPTER 2: REFLECTION QUESTIONS

- *How familiar is this relational approach to God? How does it sit with you? What arguments or experiences in your own life would contend against a relational approach to God?*

- *How have you experienced God personally in your life? How has He pursued you?*

- *As you reflect on the extent of God's love for you and His pursuit of you, how does that affect your thoughts about Him? How does it affect your feelings toward Him?*

- *What wrong thoughts or false ideas have kept you from seeking an interactive relationship with God?*

- *Whether or not you have previously had a relationship with God through Jesus, what might it look like for you to respond to God's invitation to relationship in this season of your life?*

Responding in Relationship

As we have seen, God has taken the initiative to re-establish relationship with us because He *is* relationship. If God invites us into a relationship with Himself, then the question is how do we respond? He has done all that is necessary to create the opportunity; we need only to accept His invitation and respond in relationship.

There is a temptation in modern Christianity to become so concerned with saving people's souls that we stop there. We somehow begin to act as if becoming a member of the Body of Christ was the end of the story rather than the beginning. Once people express a commitment to Christ, we welcome them to the club and suppose they can take it from there on their own. We essentially ignore them and assume they are fine and growing just because they are present at a meeting or participating in activities. Can you imagine a marriage like that?

Imagine that a man sees a woman, falls in love with her and sets out to win her love. He woos her with acts of kindness, pulling out all the romantic stops to gain her attention and affection. He responds to her resistance with determined tenderness, pursuing until she finally, blissfully, returns his love. She falls in love with him and they have a sweet courtship leading up to a wonderful wedding.

Their marriage ceremony is delightful and their honeymoon is a joyous expression of shared love and intimacy.

Now, imagine they return to the home they will make together. Instead of continuing the romantic and attentive love of their courtship, he neglects her. He produces a list of things that he expects for her to accomplish each day, and ignores her as he goes about his business. It is not difficult to imagine what would happen in that kind of relationship: what was carefully cultivated and constructed during courtship would wither and waste away, eventually dying from neglect. The couple may continue to live together for years, but their passionate romance would slowly disintegrate until they are merely room-mates. They may remain committed to one another for any number of reasons – all the while missing the bliss that could be theirs.

I know how easy it is to take a spouse for granted. I also know that much more is available. When I remember what is available and apply myself to intentionally cultivate my relationship with my wife, it flourishes. Rather than just remembering the sweet memories of our youthful courtship, I can take present delight in the wife of my youth. I can choose to invest in the relationship, to hope for more and pursue it with the intensity that may have flagged in the day-to-day grind of life. Taking love for granted is even easier in our relationship with God, and the consequences are more dire.

As I work with people, I frequently ask, "What are you doing to intentionally develop your relationship with God?" Their answers are revealing. Some cannot answer the question at all. The subject itself seems foreign to their way of thinking about God and they can't quite get their heads around it. It's as if thinking of God in relational terms is something strange. Other people will respond defensively and tell me about their church attendance or spiritual disciplines. Still others will deflect the question by changing the subject to a theological problem or practical issue they are facing in their life. Like the woman at the well, we may find it easier to debate theology than to talk honestly about the heart of the matter.[44]

On the one hand, entering into a relationship with God is fairly straightforward. It is a relatively simple message that young children can understand and personally embrace. On the other hand, the simplicity of the message can lead us to oversimplify the process of growth. Saying, "I do" is easy, but developing a healthy a marriage relationship takes time and energy.

Our relationship with God must be intentionally cultivated or it will wither and waste away. It is sometimes easier to keep up the veneer of Christian piety than to really wrestle with God and delve into the depths of our relationship. Paul warns us against having a form of godliness that is absent the power.[45] Sometimes diving in will force us to face issues we would rather leave alone, and confront problems we wish we could ignore.

It's too easy to exchange the gift of God for idols.[46] Not all of our idols are repellent to our Christian sensibilities. In fact, some of the most dangerous ones are applauded. How often do we bow down to the idol of men's praise in our lives or ministry? How often do we take our identity from our performance rather than resting in God's unconditional love? It's not hard to subtly become a modern – or should I say post-modern? – Pharisee. Jesus invited the Pharisees to come to Him, but they preferred to study their Scriptures while refusing to accept God in their midst.[47] Our Christian activity can subtly crowd out our actual relationship with God. This is the root of all Pharisaical pseudo-piety.

Perhaps another relational analogy will help. Sometimes I think of our dynamic relationship with God like parenting. If I parent my teenage daughter the same way I parent my ten-year-old son, I do her a disservice. If I parent her the same way I parented her when she was two, or even nine, that also won't work. She's growing up.

We had a sweet relationship when she was a toddler, and although our relationship today is different, it is still sweet. Often when we face difficulties, we fall back on the things we have previously learned or experienced. Learning from experience isn't necessarily bad; however, we are constantly changing and entering into new seasons where the old patterns and approaches may not apply in the same ways. Each season of life brings unique challenges and opportunities that may require a new perspective or approach.

It can be painful and scary to let go of the past and move into the unknown. A few years ago, my daughter came to us weeping and insisting she didn't want to grow up. Something had changed, and she had gained new freedom but also new responsibility. She knew the sweetness we had shared, but she could not yet imagine the sweetness that was coming. She wanted to cling to the past, to what she knew, to the familiar.

God is not only the perfect spouse, He is also the perfect parent.[48] He is the perfect friend.[49] He is the perfect brother.[50] At various points in our relationship with Him, different relational nuances will come to the fore. These subtle shifts in the relationship can be disorienting because we may not always have points of reference to help us understand the new stage. Like my daughter, we may decide we want to 'stay young and not grow up.' God is too good to allow that. He knows what is in store, even if we don't. He is teaching us to trust Him and to follow His lead to venture out into the unknown. We need to hear His voice and follow Him.[51]

Another problem we face is that those around us may not be equipped to help us on the next leg of our journey. Depending on our tradition or particular stream of Christianity, our friends or leaders may not be able to provide the direction we need for the next stage. As a pastor, I have to confess that I often default to encouraging people to grow in the ways that I have grown. When I found a particular book helpful, I recommended the book to everyone. When I found a spiritual discipline fruitful, I told anyone who came to me in need of guidance to try that practice. It's not that the lessons I'm learning are not valid or important, but when I make my journey normative for other people, I may actually hamper the growth God has in store for them.

I have grown to think of my pastoral role as analogous to a marriage counselor. I have done a fair bit of pre-marital and marital counseling in my ministry. When counseling couples, it is important to listen carefully to both people. My primary task is to help them communicate with one another. If I make the session about me and my relational experiences, I have stolen from them. They don't need to know about my marriage, they need to grow in theirs. I need to listen well to both of them and help them hear one another. Where there is error or misunderstanding of basic principles, I may also need to teach; however, the primary focus of the session is on their relationship.

My role as a pastor is similar to this. I need to listen well to the person coming to me for help in their relationship with God. I also need to listen to the Holy Spirit and seek to discern what He may be doing in and around them, or saying to them. I do my best to get the two of them to talk with and listen to each other. Obviously, the Holy Spirit doesn't need any coaching, but often we do. As a coach, I ask questions and seek to help people discover their own unique journey toward intimacy with God.

It is difficult for us to move toward the reality of this relational approach to God, as there is an almost overwhelming cultural momentum pushing us toward a systematic approach to God. Western society has programmed us to think in systemic or mechanical terms rather than relational and organic ones. I find myself constantly drifting back toward a philosophical or academic approach to God rather than an interactive one. It seems I want to reduce God to a means to meet my ends, rather than holding

Him up as the end in Himself. I want to know what He requires of me so that I can get what I want from Him. This approach betrays the relational nature of God.

Establishing and cultivating our relationship with God is foundational – the first and most important thing. All other aspects of our personality and life begin to fall into place once this cornerstone has been laid. Until that base is established, nothing else can be made truly right.

People experience need on many levels and brush against our lives in their pursuit of these needs. Frequently, people will come to me about a problem they are having or a need they feel, but the visible problem is often the manifestation of something deeper. We must not miss the opportunity to point them to their deepest need even while we care for their more superficial needs. We are not truly caring for people when we help them to mask the symptoms of their fatal disease. We can superficially treat a wound, while the cancer beneath the surface remains.

For example, a friend confides in me that he cannot seem to stop arguing with his wife. The felt need is for mediation, or marital counseling. Meeting that need is not bad, but if we are willing to dig beneath the surface, we may discover that there are deeper needs driving the marital problems. Perhaps some childhood trauma is driving present insecurities inhibiting trust and intimacy in the marriage. Alternatively, perhaps the presenting issue is an addiction of some kind. Helping to overcome the addiction is good, but even better is to help them to see the addictive behavior as symptomatic of a deeper need.

God alone can meet our deepest needs. As we become rooted and established in His love, our perspective changes – new avenues for growth, healing, and joy become available to us.[52] In and through this relationship with God we become heirs to the Kingdom of heaven and partakers in the divine nature. We receive all that we need for life and godliness.[53] Our relationship with God is the most important thing about us.

It really is all about our relationship with God! As our connection with God deepens, our souls are enlarged. Our capacity for love increases. Our ability to understand and accept ourselves as we are, and as we can be, grows. As this happens, our ability for community expands as well.

CHAPTER 3: REFLECTION QUESTIONS

- *Where are you in developing your relationship with God? Are you just getting to know Him? Are you in a committed relationship with Him?*

- *How are you relating to God in your life right now? What are you doing to intentionally develop your relationship with God?*

- *Which of His relational facets finds the most resonance in your soul? King? Father? Brother? Counselor? Which aspect might need to be further developed?*

- *What needs are you experiencing? How might these needs move you toward God?*

Relearning to Relate

Jesus said that the greatest commandment is to love God with all you are. He went on to say that the second greatest commandment is to love your neighbor as yourself. He further clarified His teaching by stating that all of the Old Testament law and the writings of the prophets hang on these two commands.[54] These are not tangential issues. Loving God and loving people are the most important things we can do!

God designed us for community – for *The Divine Community* – but we do not know how to commune even though we have been learning about the way the world works since infancy. We have been taught how to relate by our family, our culture, and our experience; unfortunately, many of the lessons were unhelpful half-truths or even lies. We have been fed lies about God, about ourselves, and about the world in which we live. The problem is that the lies don't feel like lies because they are so familiar and often have a thin veneer of truth on the surface. The most effective lies are those wrapped in half-truths. Our families and society shape our worldview in ways we are not generally aware of because they are constantly self-referential and self-reinforcing. Only a very strange fish knows it swims in water.

Sherwood Lingenfelter, noted Christian anthropologist, says that cultures are prisons of disobedience because they teach us to believe and behave in ways that are contrary to the loving will of God.[55] Our families, our schools, and our churches all teach us what to believe. However, that does not mean they are teaching us what is true. They teach from within a worldview that will not correlate with truth in every particular.

For example, God values each individual. He designed and created each human on purpose.[56] He loves and redeems us individually. However, His love for the individual is not an isolated truth; it is a part of a larger truth. God redeems individuals to integrate us into a community, the family of God.[57]

In the West, we have exalted the individual at the expense of the community. America has taken this view further than any other society I have seen. We have taught ourselves how to stand on our own two feet through the principle of self-reliance, but the unintended consequence is a culture of selfishness and self-centeredness that is rapidly deteriorating into widespread isolation. God tells us, "It is not good for the man to be alone."[58] The specific context of the passage was in the creation of the second human, but the general principle is much broader than simply a marriage relationship. We need companionship for the journey. Although we were made for human and divine companionship, we do not inherently embrace this. We have to relearn to relate.

We must recover the lost art of relating. John Donne rightly observed, "No man is an island, entire of itself."[59] We are designed for interdependence. This is true not only in our dependence on God, but also in our dependence on one another. God has placed every creature in a constant state of dependence. We are continually reminded of our dependence upon other things for our survival. If you need a quick illustration of your perpetual state of dependence, try holding your breath and see if you can live independent of air.

God gives us the gifts we need to learn the lessons we require: the gift of community that we might learn how to relate, and the gift of His Spirit that we might learn from Him. These two kinds of relationship are constantly interwoven. We cannot grow in our relationship with God while simultaneously remaining isolated from His people. It is in our relationship with God that we learn how to relate to people, and in our relationships with people that we learn how to relate to God.

In community, we can learn how to give and receive love in healthy ways. Some of us received this gift from our family; but in our increasingly fractured world, many of us did not. Many of us experienced abuse or neglect at the hands of our parents, and these wounds remain with us into our adulthood. Even those of us from stable, loving families have not had perfect parents. We are all in need of healing; it's just a question of how much. Within a loving Christian community, we can find godly men and women who can serve as more Christ-like parental models. Paul specifically directs the older members of the community to instruct the younger.[60] We can be re-parented in community.[61]

In community, we can learn to trust again. We can find safe people and safe places to let down our guard and be ourselves. Our families and our societies have encouraged us to don masks that fit the roles we are assigned, but often these masks do not reflect who we really are. Within community, we can begin to make ourselves vulnerable to one another in an attitude of love and mutual submission. We can begin to experience what trust feels like.

What about when community fails us? What about the times when we make ourselves vulnerable and are wounded again? Anyone who has spent time in real community will tell you this is bound to happen. There is no perfect community on this earth because there are no perfect people. We are all bent in one way or another. In community, we learn to give and receive forgiveness, which includes forgiveness for others as well as forgiveness for ourselves. Although those we love will likely disappoint us, we choose to love and forgive; we choose to offer grace anyway and in doing so we help to create the community we long for.

In community, we learn how to relate to each other and discover how far we have to grow. As we do so, we are healed. On the other hand, if God chooses to heal us directly via our relationship with Him, the community becomes the place for this healing to be expressed and tested. These experiences of human love, trust, and forgiveness, are a part of the divine plan for wholeness and healing. As we begin to experience these things on a human level, we can experientially understand the divine attributes of which these are but a pale reflection. Community is a part of God's plan for us and for the world.

Western individualism implies that we can grow in our relationship with God on our own. This is not at all a biblical way of thinking. In fact, all of Scripture was written to the community, or with the community in mind.[62] God deals with families, nations, and other forms of community, not only individuals. Of course, He relates to individuals as a part of that process, but the idea of a lone believer making his way in the world is foreign to the Scriptures.[63] All of Scripture points to the people of God.

In our age of hyper-mobility and the kind of shallow connections facilitated by the Internet, many are desperate for real community. The Internet trains us to present only a carefully selected portion of ourselves. Online, we edit our public persona and cautiously select our masks. Only by engaging in each other's lives across time do we really get to know each other. This is not done best from a distance. It will not happen by attending a service for an hour a week. We need to share our lives with one another. We need to be in one another's homes and in one another's business to develop the kind of community that will facilitate our growth and our relationship with God.

For some of us, community will be readily available, but for most of us, formation of community will be a process. Community is cultivated. It grows over time. We are unlikely to simply stumble across it; instead, we must choose to create it. We may shrink from the hard work of creating community unless we believe it is necessary. We will likely be hurt in the process; nevertheless, to fail to embrace community is to fail to obey the law of love and to choose less than His highest and best.[64]

We need to involve other people in our growth as well as invest in theirs. I strongly recommend involving someone else in your relationship with God. Find at least one person with whom you can begin to open up, to develop a heart-level friendship. The Celtic saints could not conceive of a growing Christian without a 'soul friend' – someone who was available to help them deal with their deep issues.[65] There is a desperate need for soul friends in the Church today.[66]

We do not naturally know how to relate to one another in a healthy way – even less do we know how to relate to God. There has probably never been a time when community was more necessary and less available. The community of God is the hope of the world, as Jesus expressed in His prayer for the Church.[67]

Our world is sick. Healthy Christian communities can transform us as individuals and serve as agents of transformation in society. Like pebbles in a rock tumbler, our rough edges rub up against others and become smooth; so too the community becomes the context in which we are polished and refined. Eventually, we become people ready to obey Jesus' command to love our neighbors and inject health into the world. This earth needs people who live and look like Jesus. We can do even greater things than He did, if we learn to love God with all we are, and to love people as we love ourselves.[68]

It is not enough to simply ponder the barriers we find in our lives and our relationship with God. Freedom in Christ is our rebirthright.[69] We have to choose to fight for it. We have to choose a new way of living, an eternal way – a way that expresses His Kingdom and His will.[70]

We take this journey together. We have to keep moving. We miss out when we choose to camp along the way or take painful detours. We have to choose to get up and keep moving forward.[71] When we do, we will find He is right there with us, our constant companion who has never left us or forsaken us.[72] As we journey with Him, we will get to know His heart. As we get to know Him, we increasingly become who we are.

CHAPTER 4: REFLECTION QUESTIONS

- *What have you previously believed or experienced about the importance of community in your relationship with God?*

- *What aspects are you missing of the freedom and eternal life that Jesus promised? How might community help you to grow into that kind of life?*

- *Do you have a community of believers that can help you to grow? If so, how can you contribute to that community? If not, what steps can you take toward creating that community?*

- *What defense mechanisms have served you well in the past but are now inhibiting your ability to connect and experience community?*

- *How readily do you offer grace and forgiveness to others? How readily do you express vulnerability and receive grace or forgiveness?*

Recovering All We Are

Jesus taught that the greatest commandment is to "…love the LORD your God with all your heart, all your soul, all your mind, and all your strength."[73] Everything starts and ends here. The question is, "How?" If the greatest commandment is to love God with all we are…then understanding what we are is critical.

In Matthew, Jesus used the words 'heart,' 'soul,' and 'mind' to capture the totality of who we are.[74] In Mark, Jesus added 'strength' to the list.[75] In the Law, which Jesus was clearly citing, we find heart, soul, and strength.[76] Whatever words we use to express it, the clear meaning is that we must love God with all we are.

The preceding chapters have largely addressed our understanding of God and our relationship with Him as well as others. These are important truths; however, I also believe that many of our problems stem from an inadequate or erroneous understanding of who we are. Jesus taught that we would do even greater things than He did – but we settle for less than this glorious life with Him.[77]

God has intentionally created each and every one of us and He knows us intimately.[78] He created each of us as a masterpiece.[79] He measured out to each of us particular gifts and aspects of His glorious image.[80] We were each created on purpose and given unique gifts and skills to accomplish good things on this earth.[81] When we say this, we are not praising or exalting ourselves. We are merely agreeing with God and praising His handiwork as the masterful Creator. God has endowed us with incredible power that is only fully activated in partnership with Him.[82] When we recognize this truth and choose to live in communion with Him, we will experience the incredible freedom He intends for us.

As believers, we have already received all that we need for life and godliness.[83] As we walk with Him, we will be transformed from glory to glory.[84] Nevertheless, many of us walk around defeated, living as if we were not the chosen people of God.[85] God offers us freedom and tells us that the same power that raised Jesus from the dead is ours through His Spirit.[86] God has created us and saved us to do good works and has given us divine power to do these works on earth.[87]

Christ has set us free so we can live free, but we settle for a small degree of that freedom.[88] It may help us to think of freedom as a continuum rather than a fixed point. There is a range from total bondage (negative 100) to total freedom (positive 100). Zero is the point where we are barely hanging on in our struggle against sin. The freedom that Christ modeled for us is +100, but too many of us set zero as our goal. At zero, we may no longer act on our sinful desires or temptations; but Jesus offers and desires for us much more than just outward obedience.[89] We are aiming far too low.

When we grasp what God is actually offering us and begin to have His vision of ourselves, we set our sights on a higher goal. We will not suddenly jump from −100 to +100, but we can collaborate with the Spirit to progress up the continuum. As we do so, we will look more and more like Christ.[90] God actually promises to

work everything in our lives toward this end, to make us look like
Christ.[91] Embracing this truth is an important step toward seeing
ourselves as God sees us. This change of perspective opens up new
possibilities for our growth.

Imagine an alcoholic: At −100, he is in total bondage to his
addiction. He doesn't have the power to choose not to drink. The
choice to drink is barely even a conscious option. He lives in his
addiction as the only possible reality. Now imagine him at zero.
At zero, he is no longer getting drunk, but it is a terrible struggle.
He notices every potential source of alcohol as he walks through
life. He feels the tug of the addiction, yet manages to maintain
his sobriety. His warped perspective on alcohol remains, even if
he manages to resist the temptation to drink. Such a life is a
continually exhausting struggle.

God intends more than this half measure of freedom. A
person living in full freedom (+100) has a completely different
relationship with alcohol. He can choose to drink or not to drink.
He is walking through life with God, filled and controlled by the
Spirit.[92] Drunkenness doesn't appeal to him because he has found
something much better – the fullness of life with Christ.[93] To be
sure, even when walking closely with the Father, we can still be
tempted. Christ was.[94] However, the more satisfied we are in God,
the less thirsty we are for our sin.[95]

We are all sin-oholics. We are all addicted to sin. Although the
particularities of our sin differ wildly, we are all in recovery. We have
to admit that we are powerless in ourselves and that God alone can
restore us to sanity and set us free.[96] This vision of freedom is the life
Jesus modeled for us. The Spirit within us makes it possible. We don't
need to simply gut it out until we are set free in heaven. We don't
need to settle for zero. Zero is much better than −100, but we can
push through to greater freedom. This process takes time, energy,
and intentionality. It is the process of growing in our relationship

with God, learning to hear His voice and to follow Him.[97] There
will be challenges and barriers along the way, but let's fix our eyes
on the prize...let's embark on the adventure! Let us spend the rest
of our lives growing in freedom...cultivating intimacy with the God
Who made us.

As mentioned before, God made us in Their image. We are
unique in all of creation in that regard. Only humans are made in
Their image. There are many differences between humans and God,
but They made us in Their image. We are like Them in some key
ways. We are relational like They are. We can think, choose, and feel
as They do. We have a body like the Son and a spirit like the Spirit.

What I want to share with you is a paradigm I have found to be
of great practical use in my personal life as well as in my ministry
to others. I do not claim it is entirely original. I owe much to many
as it has developed in my heart and mind. I call this paradigm *The
Five Circles*. Essentially, it is a way of understanding who we are.
It is my attempt to describe a holistic paradigm to help us develop
as people in relationship with God. This tool integrates various
approaches that have been helpful for me and for those I have served
through the years.

I believe that God made us as fully integrated people – body,
soul, and spirit. Often, particularly in the West, we tend to separate
these aspects of who we are, and deny in practice – if not in theory
– the interconnectedness of these areas. *The Five Circles* paradigm
has developed as I have reflected on Scripture, my own growth, and
my ministry to the whole person.

I would like to offer one caveat before I go any further. While
I am a student of the Bible and theology, my intention is not to
drive a divisive theological position with this paradigm, either as a
whole or in any of its parts. Rather, my intention is to introduce a
framework that I have found useful to promote spiritual formation
and to overcome barriers in our journey toward and with Christ.

Regardless of your theological persuasion, I believe this paradigm can be useful, as it is more pastoral than theological in intent.

I would hope for and expect you to measure it against Scripture like the noble Bereans of old.[98] Within the confines of Scripture, considerable latitude exists in some areas. If some of my particular positions are outside of your comfort zone, do not allow that to invalidate the entire model. Please look past any of my particular positions to the larger paradigm and see if it might be of use in your life or in the lives of those to whom you minister.

The Five Circles is a visual or mental aid I have found helpful as I consider where problems or barriers might lie in our relationship with God. Each circle represents a part of us as a human being, created by God in His image. Each one of us has a body, a soul, and a spirit. For the sake of clarity, in this model, I have portrayed the soul components – the mind, will, and emotions – as distinct facets of our being. **Figure 1** is a visual representation of this paradigm.

THE FIVE CIRCLES

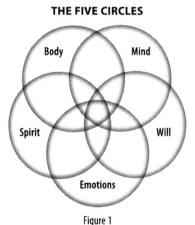

Figure 1

As the figure indicates, these parts of us are not separate from one another; they are interconnected. These connections are rarely isolated to just one or two parts of who we are. Rather, there is a dynamic network of interactions constantly taking place within us. I attempt to represent this by overlapping the circles. Toward the outer edges of the model, you find the isolated aspects of our personhood. As you move toward the center, these areas overlap with first one, then two, then three, and finally all four other portions of our being. The resulting picture is one where each part of who we are is integrated and interacting with every other part.

In practice, it is difficult to identify the dividing lines between these various aspects. How does one clearly differentiate between the emotions and the mind, or between the mind and the spirit? I am not attempting to drive a particular philosophical agenda in understanding or defining these various areas. I have found that these 'layman's' terms help us think more clearly about how we can identify potential sources for problems we are facing and minister more effectively to others. This paradigm also helps to identify potential avenues of growth in our relationship with God.

We were designed to love God with all we are. We were created to relate with all five of these parts of ourselves. To fail to do so is to disobey the greatest commandment. We cannot hold parts of ourselves back without damaging our relationship with God, which damages our relationships with others and inhibits our own growth.

Many models for growth emphasize one or more areas and may even address them very well; however, they often do so at the expense of another area. For example, some ministries emphasize knowledge. They may quote, "You will know the truth, and the truth will set you free."[99] They emphasize the mind. This approach is not a bad thing; in fact, it is critical that we rightly understand ourselves, God, and the world around us. However, if they also denigrate psychological help or spiritual warfare ministries, their emphasis lacks balance. In their overemphasis of knowledge, they have denied the importance of other aspects of our humanity.

The Five Circles describes the core components of our being, and guides us as we consider practical steps toward growth. Our mind is one part of who we are, but we cannot stop at simple acknowledgement. In order to grow, we need to ask if we are using our mind properly. Are we thinking rightly? We know we have a will and we use it regularly, but are we making right choices? What is happening in our emotions? Are our feelings aligned with what is actually true? Have we considered the spiritual aspect? Have we sought spiritual freedom? How about the physical component? Are we honoring our body? These types of questions can help us move from the abstract paradigm toward application. **Figure 2** shows a slightly different rendering of *The Five Circles* meant to move us beyond information toward application.[100]

THE FIVE CIRCLES

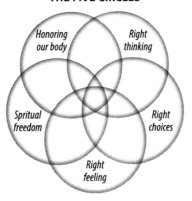

Figure 2

The Five Circles is meant to help us think about the whole person and to intentionally seek to help the whole person. When someone comes to me with a problem, it is rarely isolated to just one aspect of his or her being; or if it started in one aspect, the ramifications have often spread to include other areas.

Imagine finding a young woman lying on the street. As you stop to help, you discover she is bleeding. Your first step would likely be to stop the bleeding. As you do so, she reveals that her cuts and bruises are from the beating her father just gave her. What seemed at first to be a problem with her body has very quickly come to encompass her emotions and likely other aspects of who she is as well.

Alternatively, imagine that a young man confides in you that he is addicted to pornography. He is a Christian and has tried to stop, but has failed miserably. Depending on our background, we might suggest Scripture memorization, a Bible study on purity, or a word study on the use of the Greek word 'porneo' in the New Testament. These would suggest that we think the problem is primarily one of wrong thinking and our advice would move him toward right thinking. On the other hand, we might suggest that he make better choices about environment, friendships, or problematic patterns of behavior. In this case, we would be encouraging him to exercise his will as a means to change. Another option would be that of counseling or inner healing. In these cases, you would be locating the problem as an emotional one. Some people would immediately want to deliver the young man from the spirit of lust and might call for spiritual warfare prayer and not giving the devil a foothold. This person would see the problem as falling into the spiritual area.

Sometimes the solutions we suggest are just the right answer for the person to whom we are ministering, but sometimes we miss the mark. Most of us minister to others based on our own experience; we make suggestions based on what has been helpful in our own lives or in the lives of those around us. In other words, we repeat what we have seen or heard. That's not a bad thing; however, depending on what experiences we have had, our advice will vary wildly and may not be at all useful to the person we seek to help.

People are incredibly diverse and our backgrounds are so varied that the problems we face deserve more than a 'one size fits all' solution. Whether we are working on our own issues or helping someone else, we need to ask questions and listen carefully to the answers. *The Five Circles* can guide us in asking questions, gaining insight, rightly understanding problems, identifying potential solutions, and suggesting practical steps toward healing, wholeness, and intimacy with God.

We need to be careful to remember that our relationship with God is the core pursuit. God is the One who heals and frees as we draw near to Him. If we make our goal wholeness, healing, or freedom, those goals can subtly become our idols. It is not that freedom is a bad goal, but it is not the ultimate one. I have found that as we grow closer to God we become more whole and free. We become like the thing we behold, the thing we exalt, the thing we worship.[101] He made us for relationship with Him, and each aspect of who we are is important to that relationship. We cannot be content just to do what comes easy to us. Growing in relationship with God means embracing all of who God made us to be, and striving to become who we are. As we do that, freedom results.

Only human beings have to struggle to become who we are. Other creatures do not have a choice about what they become. Trees grow without making conscious choices. Only humans think about what we would like to become. We make decisions that affect the direction of our lives.[102] The flip side of this is our capacity to stunt ourselves. We have the capacity for denial. We can choose to move into or withdraw from relationship. Sometimes these are conscious decisions and other times we choose them without realizing why. By pursuing God, we can cultivate awareness. We can choose to love God with all we are, leaving nothing out and holding nothing back.[103] When we fail to love God with our mind, our will, our emotion, our spirit, or our body, we are failing in the most basic, the most central command – the command to love God with all we are.

As children of God, we are more glorious, powerful, and free than we can conceive. We are also more weak, needy and dependent than we care to admit. The more I get to know our gracious God as He really is, the more I am willing to admit the dark parts and embrace the glorious parts of who I am. Countless times in the Old

Testament, the Lord sent His people into battle, but He didn't send them alone. He promised to go with them. I can only imagine the fear and trepidation of suiting up for a battle that cannot be won if God doesn't come through.

We face battles like that in our lives, even within ourselves. When we choose to confront the enemy and invite God to rescue us, He comes through. He really is for us. He really is with us. He really is mighty to save. The hard part is to live this way: believing He really is who He is and we really are who He says we are.

CHAPTER 5: REFLECTION QUESTIONS

- *How well are you obeying the greatest commandment, loving God with every part of your being?*

- *In what ways have you been settling for less than the best God has for you?*

- *Where would you put yourself on the freedom continuum? What steps can you take to move toward greater freedom?*

- *How comfortable are you with the paradigm of The Five Circles? Are any of The Five Circles new to you? Is there one you have failed to recognize or explore in the past?*

- *What areas of yourself have you developed well? What area might be a focus for future exploration and growth?*

PART TWO

Becoming Who We Are

My Journey Through 'The Five Circles'

Accepting God's invitation to relationship with Him is the beginning of a beautiful adventure. As we launch out into the voyage of discovering God, we are also embarking on a journey of self-discovery. As we draw near to Him, He will shape us into His likeness in every aspect of our being.

In **Part Two**, we'll be looking at each of *The Five Circles* in more depth. As we do so, I want us to keep in mind the interconnectedness of the circles.

I often use the hand as an example of this blend of individuality and interdependence. We have five fingers on each hand. Each finger has its own identity and can be used separately to a certain degree. However, if you hold your hand out in front of you (palm toward you) and attempt to touch just one finger to your palm, you will see that it pulls the other fingers – forcing them to move. Then, turn your hand over and see the tendons tug at one another on the back of your hand as you move each finger 'independently.' The various parts of your hand work as a unit, not merely as individual parts. What is true for our hands is true for our whole being as well.

Paul paints oddly funny word pictures of the individual parts of the body trying to operate independently of one another.[104] It is ludicrous to think of one part of our body declaring independence from another part of our body and surviving. This concept of interdependence is found in our physical body, in our humanity, throughout creation, and even in the value that the Scriptures place on community. This interdependence finds its source in the very nature of the Triune God, eternally existing in interdependent community.

My Story

Perhaps sharing how this model has been helpful in my own journey will illustrate its usefulness. In my first book, I told the story of God's pursuit of me.[105] I emphasized the aspects of the story that best illustrated God's interventions in His relentless quest to save me. Along the way, He taught me about the five components of my humanity. My story is a real-life illustration of how these five parts of me all play an important role in my journey with God, and toward God.

I grew up in a conservative Christian context in America. I knew a lot about God. From a young age, my mind was filled with biblical images and information, providing a strong knowledge foundation that has helped me tremendously through the years. I was given a fully-formed worldview that I assumed was all true, and much of it actually was. On closer examination, I've found some gaps. Some areas that then seemed black and white now have more shades of gray than I was led to believe. Nevertheless, I am grateful for the grounding I received in the church. I was taught about the primacy of Scripture and received a lot of helpful instruction.

The development of my mind was also aided by my family and by the education I received. My parents valued reading and thinking. We often had lively discussions about ideas and current events around the table. I was encouraged to study hard in school (not that I always did) and to think critically.

I was also privileged to grow up in a family that taught me personal discipline. Early on, my parents instilled in me the importance of accepting responsibility for my choices. I understood that my choices mattered and that exercising my will was a part of life. Bringing my will into submission was a later challenge, but I am grateful I learned the lessons of personal choice and responsibility early in life.

My family and my faith community did not prepare me well in other ways. We did not talk about feelings or emotions much at all. Instead, we were told to know the truth and to live accordingly. Emotions were fickle things and not to be trusted. I remember being emphatically told, "Only really crazy people need counseling and no one in our family is crazy!" There were only two things that mattered: 1 – knowing what was right; and, 2 – doing it. If you had any problems executing point two, see point one. It was all very black and white.

When I was twelve, I chose to trust someone in the church who was untrustworthy and who severely hurt me. I was unprepared for this. I don't suppose any child is prepared for abuse. In the years that followed, I had nowhere to go with the pain, nowhere safe to process the emotions. This hidden hurt became a driving force in my life. I began to make a series of compounding bad choices. In the language of addiction, I chose to self-medicate. I chose alcohol, drugs, and sexual gratification as the means to escape from the pain in my soul. Each time I did, I found temporary relief that only compounded the damage.

During my teen years, I continued to attend church because I was required to by my parents, but I found no help there for my journey. I'm sure there were trustworthy people who would have been willing to help me if I had let them, but the scared child within wouldn't let anyone get close. I walled myself off emotionally and was stuck behind those walls for years, even as I continued to gain more knowledge through consistent church attendance.

Ultimately, God used my intellect to draw me to Himself. In my first year of university, I began to seriously search for truth. I looked into various worldviews and belief systems, comparing them to one another and the world around me. I started my journey by rejecting Christianity. However, to be intellectually honest with myself I felt I had to include an investigation of the person of Christ, if only to permanently exclude Him. In the end, I was arrested by the picture of Jesus Christ portrayed in the Gospels. I could not fail to see that He was truly the Son of God and worthy of my allegiance. It was at this critical juncture that my spirit was renewed and engaged. The information I'd taken in had remained mere information. It wasn't until my heart was changed and my spirit revived that I began to actually love God. I had returned to the Father, but my journey was far from over.

I had made the crucial choice. I had chosen God and pledged myself to Him; however, I little understood the implications of that decision. Although I had experienced a change of heart, I continued to struggle in overcoming my addiction to self-medication. I did not know which way to turn. God provided a friend who encouraged me to consider counseling. I immediately rebuffed the suggestion, but he was not easily put off. As he openly shared his journey with me, I was intrigued and began to hope that counseling might help.

I entered into counseling with quite a few reservations about its usefulness in general and in my life in particular. Imagine my surprise when I began to find relief from my compulsions and the hurt that had driven me all those years! To my dismay, as I began to examine my internal life, I found there were more subtle wounds that had been festering from my childhood as well. With the help of a Christian counselor, I explored the tender places in my soul and found tremendous healing. I found that dealing with the emotional and relational roots of my pain created long-sought freedom in my attitudes and behavior. Over the years, I had blamed others for my problems and temptations. Now, I found that the problems really had been coming from within all these years.[106] I had to adjust my worldview to encompass the emotional aspect of my humanity.

It was around this same time that I began to live my life more vulnerably and to seek to develop real community. I was realizing that some of the lessons of counseling could also be experienced in community. As I did so, I found healing in and through authentic community. I found men who modeled an integrated and passionate pursuit of God for me, and I found brothers and sisters who were on similar quests for intimacy with Him. Some were farther along than I was, while others were walking a few steps behind. I began to learn how to journey alongside people and serve them.

During this same season of my life, I had to broaden my understanding again to include the spiritual dynamics involved. I was exposed to teaching on our identity in Christ and the reality of spiritual opposition.[107] This was all new to me. I had been taught virtually nothing about this whole area. Whenever this topic came up, I had been assured that those portions of Scripture did not apply to me because, "Christians cannot be attacked or influenced by demons." However, as I studied the Bible for myself, I found the argument had no scriptural validity. I tested the principles of spiritual warfare in the laboratory of life, and found that they actually worked.[108]

Many of my bad choices had opened up doors in my life through which Satan and his minions had access. It was a fairly straightforward process to figure out which doors had been opened and then to shut them. It has been a longer journey to cultivate awareness and consistently live in the authority that God has delegated to His children.

It was during this period that I first began to explore the ideas that have matured into *The Five Circles*. At the time, there were four quadrants and not five circles because I did not ascribe much significance to the body. It was in ministering to others that I began to realize the importance of our physicality. God has blessed me with a remarkably low-maintenance body. I had never realized this, since

I had nothing with which to compare it. As I began to share life with others, and particularly after I was married, I realized that in some cases the physical is a major factor. As I explored this with others I began to reflect on how my body, or more specifically the neglect and abuse of it, had impeded my journey. I started to understand that our pursuit of God had to include all that made us human; and so the fifth facet of our humanity was included in the model.

As I have grown into this understanding of myself and of God, I have discovered that our relationship has a new footing. The more I experience God as He really is, the more I come to understand who I really am. Only God sees me as I really am in every aspect of my being, and He loves me unconditionally. In and through my relationship with God, I find out more about myself. The more I experience and trust His loving intentions toward me, the more I am willing to face the depths of my soul. I continue to struggle and to face barriers and obstacles in my journey. I continue to make sinful choices and am forced to explore the attitudes and behaviors that drive me toward the cisterns.[109] My journey is not over, but I'm pressing on.[110]

As we examine each facet of our humanity individually – as well as the interactions between them – I hope you will discover new avenues to intimacy with God. As you learn to love God with every part of your being, you will find yourself transforming and continuing your journey to become who you are.

CHAPTER 6: REFLECTION QUESTIONS

- *To what parts of my journey can you best relate?*
  Are there parts that you had trouble connecting with?

- *Which of* The Five Circles *have been most significant*
  in your journey? How have they been significant?

- *Which of* The Five Circles *have not been a significant*
  part of your awareness during your life journey so far?

- *How have you experienced the interconnectedness*
  of The Five Circles *in your life?*

THE SPIRIT
Finding Spiritual Freedom

Jesus said, "For God is Spirit, so those who worship him must worship in spirit and in truth."[111] The spiritual aspect of our being is perhaps the most difficult to grasp, but it is actually the point of departure for our journey. Until we come alive spiritually, we cannot commune with God. This revival of our spirits is commonly called conversion.[112]

Conversion is a mysterious process and experience. Some of us can identify a particular moment in history when we were changed; for others, the experience is more gradual. Whatever our experience has been, the Scriptures make a clear distinction between those who are spiritually alive and those who are spiritually dead, or to put it another way, those who have come to the party, and those who are still outside.[113]

I met John while working in a warehouse.[114] We didn't have much in common. I was working my way through graduate school and he was a high school dropout. Whenever he wasn't at work, and occasionally when he was, he was drunk or high. He was living with his girlfriend and had a rough persona. One day he plopped down in a chair across the table from me in the lunchroom. I was trying to catch up on some studies for class and had my Bible and some theology books strewn across the table. Everyone usually gave me a wide berth when I had my Bible out. John sat down across from me and asked me, "What's the deal with this whole Bible thing?" That was the start of a beautiful relationship.

Although John had grown up as a Catholic, he no longer attended church. He was suspicious when he found out I wasn't Catholic. He had no idea what separated Protestants and Catholics, but he knew we were on the opposite side of something. I asked if we could set our differences aside and discuss God and the parts of the Bible we held in common. He agreed that was a good idea. I suggested we start reading through the Bible, a chapter a day, and discuss it after work on Fridays. We started in the Gospels. Each Friday evening, we met at a local restaurant. I would ask him what he'd read and if anything had jumped out at him. He would invariably relate a story that touched him, a question, or a problem he had with something in the text. I did my best to point him to the text for answers or to lead him to another portion of Scripture that would provide an explanation or a broader context in which to place the specifics.

It wasn't long before he was wrestling with the identity of Jesus. He found a compelling picture of Jesus in the Gospel accounts. It was so fun for me to watch the well-worn (to me) stories shock and surprise John. I watched as the agony of the crucifixion washed over his face and as the miracle of the resurrection took hold of his emotions. One day, he asked how to follow Jesus, how to become a disciple. It was with great joy that I helped him over the threshold into the household of God.[115]

Like John, we are all desperately in need of saving. We were all dead once, and lived as walking dead men. We were physically, intellectually, emotionally, and volitionally alive, but spiritually dead.[116] In that state, we could not save ourselves any more than a dead man could open a door. Someone had to open the door, come in, and make us alive. That someone is Jesus. Those of us who have already been revived have taken a tremendous step toward becoming who we are – the most important and momentous step!

Coming alive spiritually is a part of the re-creation – the making all things new – that God is working out.[117] There is no room for pride or superiority among those who have been revived. We did nothing to merit it or produce it through our works.[118] Salvation is a great mystery. What is clear is that when we come alive, we have the ability to live in new ways; we receive the ability to experience God intimately through His Spirit.[119]

Being born again spiritually is the beginning of a new way of living. When we talk about salvation, we often talk about when we were *saved* in the past tense. But salvation is both a once-in-a-lifetime event *and* a continuing process. Sometimes we make the mistake of limiting our understanding of the Gospel to only the atonement.[120] As long as we think of salvation merely in terms of being saved from the consequences and power of sin through the death of Christ, we miss the wildness of what God is really offering us.

Once we are saved, we can begin to develop the spiritual part of ourselves. It's not just that we are saved *from* something; we are saved *for* something. We are invited to the party, invited into the family business, and invited into a marriage-like intimate relationship with the Creator and Sustainer of all things! This relationship may be many years in gestation, but conversion is the point of re-birth.[121]

A physical example might help to clarify. When a baby is born, it has all five senses: Taste, Touch, Sight, Smell, and Hearing. The senses are all active and functioning, though the baby does not know how to use or interpret the data the senses are providing. The muscles are all there, yet they still have to be developed. All of the components are alive but must be exercised to realize their potential. So too, when people are born again – spiritually resurrected – they have new capacities, and may even experience some of them immediately; however, they will have to learn how to live this new kind of life they have begun.[122]

God's created universe is more complex than we typically realize. Scientists are continually learning new things and often finding that new discoveries require them to unlearn some things they thought they knew. A similar process happens for us as we begin to live in the world as it really is. This process can be daunting; and as our eyes are opened to the spiritual dimension of life, we will discover that we have an enemy.

A few years ago, I had the privilege of leading two young men to Christ. When they decided to become His disciples, we agreed to study the Scriptures together. We read a chapter a day and then met together weekly to discuss what we had read. We started in the Gospel of Matthew to help them get to know Jesus better.

I will never forget one of our meetings. It was not uncommon for them to come with some questions written down. One question this time caught me unaware. My friend was genuinely puzzled as to why Jesus was interacting with demons all the time. He asked, "Where did the demons go? Obviously there are no demons now, but Jesus dealt with them all the time." My friend had come across something in the Scriptures that did not fit with his worldview. He was trying to make sense of it, to sort out what was true and what was false. My friend's honest question caused us all to pause, and provided the opportunity to reexamine our worldview in light of Scripture.

Few of us in the West truly live with a biblically-integrated worldview. We have unconsciously subscribed to a materialistic worldview where the only things that actually exist are physical objects. We have relegated angels and demons to the realm of myth and fairytale, even though they were clearly a part of the world of Christ. So, where did they go? Did they leave? Was Christ delusional? Or perhaps…are we delusional when we deny the reality of the spiritual world?

The fact is that God is real, and so are the devil, demons, and angels. Scripture is very clear on these points. Jesus specifically trained His disciples and gave them authority to cast out demons. This was an accepted fact of the ministry that Jesus expected His disciples to do.[123] It is also clear that we are spiritual beings every bit as much as we are physical ones! We cannot ignore the implications of this truth. Our Western culture has not adequately prepared us for the actual world. By denying the existence of the spiritual world – or at the very least denying its relevance for our lives – we have neglected a core part of our very being. We have chosen to limit our perception of reality in unhelpful ways. The spiritual dimension of our world is every bit as important and integrated as the part of our world perceived through our physical senses.

Before conversion, our ability to perceive spiritual reality was extremely limited and decidedly warped.[124] We were enslaved to the spiritually dead way of thinking. We were in bondage to sin and death, and had no chance for victory over spiritual opposition.[125] When Jesus made us alive, He freed us from sin and death.[126] He also triumphed over the spiritual forces of evil, although we still have battles to fight.[127] He has invited us to live in light of His victory. He has also drafted us into the battle. He has given us authority to deal with spiritual opposition. When we leave out the possibility of demons, we have a tendency to demonize human opponents. Paul specifically says that our real battle is against spiritual forces of wickedness in the heavenly places and not against flesh and blood.[128]

I'm not saying that there is a demon behind every bush or that we can throw up our hands as victims, blaming demons for our problems. I am saying that demons are real and that part of growing as a Christian is learning how to live *as we are* in the world *as it is*. Demons are a part of that world, as are angels. We simply can't put our heads in the sand and hope they will go away. They haven't gone away since the time of Jesus and they won't be going away in our time either. The devil is actively on the prowl and looking for people he can devour.[129] He is a liar and a destroyer. When he lies, he speaks his native tongue.[130]

In *The Art of War*, Sun Tzu says that all war is based on deception.[131] Satan has masterfully deceived the West into ignoring him and therefore he is virtually unopposed. He's a master strategist and this one tactic has effectively disarmed an entire portion of the church. We have much to learn in this area from our African, Asian, and Latin American brothers and sisters. Their cultures generally predispose them to live a more spiritually integrated life. They're not shocked to learn that the spiritual world is real; they are shocked that Christians in the West would deny this obvious truth and its implications.

I'm continually astonished to find otherwise biblically literate people denying the reality of this ongoing spiritual war. Why would Jesus teach his disciples how to deal with demons if it was something they weren't going to need to know?[132] Why would Peter write to Christians and tell them to stay alert and keep watch because the devil is out there, if he was of no consequence?[133] Why would John say that Christians overcome the devil by the blood of Christ and the Word of our testimony, if he didn't need to be overcome?[134] Why would Paul command us to stand firm and to resist the devil if we wouldn't be coming under attack?[135]

My goal here is not to write a book on spiritual warfare. Many good books addressing that subject have already been written.[136] My goal is to invite you to recognize the reality of this aspect of who you are and the world you live in. You are a spiritual being. You are either alive in Christ already or, even now, have the opportunity to choose life. If you are already a new creation in Christ, you have been entrusted with real authority to make a difference in the battle between good and evil. That battle is both within us and around us. The spiritual part of you is constantly interacting with and influencing the other parts of you even as it is being influenced by them. You ignore or neglect this reality to your own peril. You cannot become all that you are meant to be while at the same time denying this core aspect of your personhood.

When we fail to recognize the spiritual part of who we are, we leave ourselves wide open to attack. We will also fail to recognize when the source of a problem might originate in this area. Not every problem has a spiritual root; however, this aspect of us does play a role. There is not a demon behind every painful experience, but that doesn't mean that they are not behind any experiences at all. Once we begin to recognize the reality of spiritual opposition, we can learn how to deal with it. The Scriptures are filled with excellent and clear teaching about how to live in the spiritual world. Once you begin to read the Bible with this in mind, you will be amazed what you find.

Mystery permeates all facets of life, and the spiritual world is no exception. However, when we begin to take the Word of God seriously in this area, we find that it is relatively straightforward and in some ways easy to deal with. Essentially, we need to understand who we are in Christ and exercise the authority He has given us as His ambassadors – His representatives here on earth.[137] We are neither smarter nor more powerful than demons on our own, but we should not be intimidated by them or give way to fear. We serve the Creator of the universe, and as His representatives, we have nothing to be afraid of.[138] Even the gates of hell will not stand against Christ.[139] He has already won the victory. We just need to learn how to stand our ground.[140]

Scripture clearly teaches us to resist the devil, and that when we do, he will flee from us.[141] He doesn't flee because he is afraid of us; He flees because he cannot stand before Christ. Satan is no gentleman; if we do not resist him, he will not leave. That is why Paul and Peter both admonish Christians to be aware of the devil's schemes and to be on guard against him.[142] Satan and his minions hate people because we are made in the image of God. They hate God but can't destroy Him, so they attack His children. When we are not on our guard, we are more vulnerable to his attacks. Those who are not yet spiritually alive are defenseless against his advances. They are easily led astray, as we all once were.[143] Knowing this should lead us to view non-believers with compassion. They are not the enemy, nor are they to be pitied. They are now what we were before God rescued us. They are prisoners of war in the battle between good and evil. Those of us who have been freed have the duty, privilege, and obligation to wage war on their behalf. Too often, we argue through the fence of the death camp, trying to convince the emaciated prisoners that they should choose freedom. Instead, we need to work to set them free. We need to be people of prayer, interceding for them as Christ does for us all.[144]

Learning how to fight spiritually through prayer is among the most important things we can discover, having implications for our personal lives as well as for our ministry to others. Spiritual warfare is not just something out in the world; it is something in us as well.

Perhaps a personal example will help to illustrate. As I was preparing to write today, I found myself feeling despondent. I was unmotivated and more than a bit cranky. Some of that is undoubtedly emotional – my insecurities coming to the surface again. I talked this out with my wife and prayed about it. I also took a few minutes to specifically resist the devil in prayer. There was no thunder and lightning, no horror-show manifestations, but I immediately felt more freedom and clarity. It was as if a dark cloud that had been hovering over me gently blew away. Taking this action took all of thirty seconds…and the results were clear. There was a spiritual component to the problem. Had I dealt with it only on an emotional level, I would have missed the greater freedom that was available to me.

Sometimes, particularly when we are just starting to deal with this area of our lives, it is more complicated. Paul warns us not to give the devil a foothold.[145] Nevertheless, many of us have invited

him into our lives (intentionally or unintentionally) and he has
taken up residence. The process of evicting him will take more time
and energy when he has been a welcomed guest. The process is still
straightforward though. We need to identify the ways in which we
have invited his presence in our life – or at least left the doors open and
the welcome mat out – and revoke those invitations. Then we need to
lock those doors and not open them again. Learning and practicing
these truths has been revolutionary for me personally, and opened
up a new avenue of ministry to others. Over the years, my wife and I
have walked a number of people through this process of deliverance.
It is amazing to see people taste freedom…but then disheartening to
see some fall back into old patterns that enslave them again.

When Debbie walked into the room, she carried a cloud of
anger and confusion with her. She seemed unable to pull out of
it. I asked her for permission to pray for her. Once she gave it, I
took authority over the situation and commanded all evil spiritual
forces to leave in Jesus' name. The change was immediate. When
we looked up from prayer, she had been transformed. She was still
herself, but she was much more relaxed and able to focus; and the
hostility was gone. Over the next few meetings, we walked through
the process of helping her to understand and identify ways that she
might have opened the doors for demonic involvement in her life.
As she understood each area, she prayed and renounced each avenue
of potential demonic influence. As she systematically cleaned up her
spiritual house, she became lighter and happier. At the end of the
process, she was the most amazing version of herself, laughing and
joking. With great joy, we sent her on her way.

Sadly, within just a few weeks, she was back in her self-destructive
cycles. After closing all the spiritual doors during our times together,
she proceeded to reopen them. She stumbled, as we all do, but
then failed to confess, repent, and reclaim her freedom and spiritual
authority. She left herself open to attack again. An additional

problem was her unwillingness to forgive several people who had victimized her. That unforgiveness left a gaping hole in her spiritual defenses. Debbie's unhealed pain had morphed into bitterness and resentment. Although she wanted freedom, she was unwilling to give up her desire to avenge herself on those who had wounded her. In her greater desire to not free *them*, she had enslaved *herself*.

We were made for freedom, but Satan wants to enslave us. When we choose the path of destruction and deceit, rather than the path of life and truth, we are operating in a satanic way. We are essentially cooperating with Satan to see his kingdom come and his will be done on earth.[146] When we do this, we are opening the door for him to mess with us.[147]

The beautiful thing is that we don't have to live in slavery. As soon as we recognize that we have allowed ourselves to be chained up again, we can throw off the chains and reclaim our freedom through the power of the blood of Christ. It honestly breaks my heart to see people who have tasted freedom choosing to return to living in chains.

Finding freedom in the spiritual part of ourselves is perhaps the most straightforward part of our journey, if we will only grasp it and live in light of it. As this area clears up, we have greater freedom to address the other areas. Just as the other areas should not be treated in isolation, neither should this one. One of the difficulties in approaching our relationship with God holistically is that few people do so. Often experts in one area will tend to overemphasize their area of expertise to the detriment of others. As I have read and worked in this area, commonly called spiritual warfare, I have learned a lot from those who have gone before me. However, I have also found myself discouraged by some who are experienced in this arena. They seem to portray spiritual warfare as the only battle that matters – as if all problems were only because of spiritual opposition.

I have also been discouraged by the sensationalist approach to this area that makes it easier for people to be skeptical or hesitant to even explore this facet of our lives. In their zealousness to help people they have sometimes accomplished the opposite. Some of these spiritual showmen have created a kind of dependency on themselves as if they were the source of freedom. Despite the abundance of sensationalism available to us in the media, we must not allow the errors or exaggerations of some to cause us to throw the baby of freedom out with the bathwater of melodrama.

Spiritual freedom is for every born-again believer, but we must learn to claim that right and to walk in freedom. We can't just assume our spiritual freedom will come as we grow in other areas. While not treating it as the only aspect that matters, we must take it seriously. The goal is not spiritual power or authority; these are already ours. The goal is growing in our relationship with God. He is standing at the door and knocking.[148] He is inviting us to do our part to open the door, to resist the devil and to keep in step with the Spirit.[149] This aspect of our humanity is every bit as important as the others. Loving God with all we are requires us to intentionally address spiritual strongholds and walk in spiritual freedom. This is a part of the abundant life, of going into the party and feasting with Him.

Finding true spiritual freedom for the first time is a glorious mystery. Scripture uses beautiful metaphors to describe this transformation: adoption, re-birth, receiving a new heart or spirit. All of these point to the depth of transformation in conversion. Until this happens, we can't relate to God as His children. Once we have been welcomed into His family and exchanged our broken hearts for new hearts, we learn to walk in Truth. We continually dedicate ourselves to renew our minds and learn to think rightly about God, ourselves, and the world around us.

CHAPTER 7: REFLECTION QUESTIONS

- *Have you found true spiritual freedom in Christ?
  Are you alive spiritually? If so, what was your experience
  of spiritual re-birth? How did it happen for you?*

- *Have you ever considered the implications of
  the spiritual world for everyday life?*

- *How are you cultivating awareness of the spiritual world?*

- *How have you experienced the reality of spiritual warfare in your life?*

- *How familiar are you with how to engage in spiritual warfare?*

THE MIND
Finding the Truth

The Spirit of God is always at work drawing all men to the Father through the Son. I believe the Word of God is the best way to introduce people to Jesus. Therefore, the best way to help someone come to faith or to grow in their faith is to get them into the Word and trust the Spirit to guide them to the aspect of truth that is most important for them. At the beginning of the previous chapter, I introduced you to John and told you how He met God. My studies with John gave me the perfect opportunity to test this theory.

The weeks following John's surrender to Jesus were difficult for me. John continued to sleep with his girlfriend. He continued to drink, smoke, and swear like a sailor. Everything in me wanted to rebuke him and tell him how he needed to change…that his behavior was not glorifying to God. I longed to insist that he was a Christian now, and he had better start living like one. Only with great difficulty did I hold my tongue.

We continued to meet for study, and he continued to express his eagerness to grow closer to Jesus. I could see changes in his demeanor, and his girlfriend remarked that he was changing a lot and for the better. However, his lifestyle was far from Christ-like. I decided to continue to guide him toward the Word and let the Spirit do all the convicting in His perfect timing. I acknowledged that John was God's child and He could raise him as He saw fit.

After the Gospels, we decided to read Ephesians to give him a general understanding of the basic truths of Christianity. One Friday, he came into the restaurant looking somber. He sat down and immediately asked me what 'sexual immorality' meant.[150] I asked him what he thought it meant and prayed for the Spirit to guide his answer. With tears in his eyes, he said he thought it meant that he needed to stop sleeping with his girlfriend. I agreed. He then pointed out that later in the same chapter it said he shouldn't be getting drunk, either.[151] I agreed. I could see he was wrestling inside. He'd lived his whole life doing whatever he felt like doing, and now he was faced with submission.

I explained to John what I'd been learning: that God doesn't give us rules to keep us from good things. He gives us guidance about the best way to live, the way that will give us the closest relationship with Him and will be best for us as well. I told him God wasn't out to rip him off. God wanted to exchange the lesser for the greater, the worse for the best. I acknowledged it would be a step of faith to give up what he knew for the unknown. I encouraged him to follow through on what he felt God was saying and to see what happened as a result.

He asked why I hadn't told him these things before, and I told him that I wanted him to hear it directly from the Word and the Spirit, in God's timing. That way, it was an argument between him and God, rather than him and me. He smiled at that and agreed it was probably a wise course of action. Moreover, he chose immediately to submit to God. We talked about practical options for bringing his life into line with what God required of him. He decided not to sleep with his girlfriend again until they got married. They were married a week later.

John had not been living rightly because he didn't know any better. He lacked knowledge. He needed truth. As followers of Christ, we are lovers of truth. We seek truth wherever we can find it, and specifically in the Scriptures. Thinking rightly is important in our relationship with God. It is critical that we correctly understand who God is, who we are, and how we should live in the world. An authentic relationship with God must go beyond intellectual knowledge and the grasp of relevant information. However, we cannot skip this foundational step. Clearly, what we believe and teach matters.

In his book, *The Knowledge of the Holy*, A. W. Tozer suggests that our concept of God, what we understand in our minds about Him, is the most important thing about us – even more important than anything we do. This applies not only to individual Christians, but also to the community of believers, that is, the Church. How we view God matters because we tend to move toward our mental image of God.[152] This is true not only for Christians, but for all people, even for those who have no religion.

What we believe – what we truly believe about the universe – is revealed by the way we live. Ideas have power regardless of their truth or falsity. A quick glance at history bears this out. We move toward our ideal. What we believe and teach can have momentous consequences, even if those consequences are beyond our field of vision or our personal experience. There would have been no Mao without Lenin and no Lenin without Marx and Engels, and no Hitler without Nietzsche.

Today, Western society is caught in the dangerous drift toward classic American pragmatism, which tells us that what we believe is important because of the benefits of right belief or the consequences of wrong belief. Pragmatism's focus on the result of beliefs is helpful, but I believe there is a deeper value here – the value of truth itself. It is good and right to believe something because it is actually true, even if the results of the belief are not immediately gratifying. If I believe myself to be a man, this is simple fact. I don't believe that I'm a man, as opposed to a turnip, because it is beneficial to do so. I believe it because it is true. I find it necessary to comment on this because I frequently find myself drifting toward this peculiarly American pragmatism. It has been argued that pragmatism is the undergirding philosophy of American culture.[153] The idea that something is valuable only to the extent that it betters one's life was clearly expressed by William James,[154] and is now the foundation of the dominant Western worldview, which is progressively becoming more and more pervasive around the globe. James and the other American Pragmatists would have us define truth as those things that are useful for our concrete life – things that produce a clear and present benefit.

This presumes that we are in a position to understand what is truly beneficial – what is best for our world and us. They would have us sit in judgment, deciding which parts of Scripture or attributes of God are particularly useful for us, and then ascribe truth only to those; anything else is viewed as 'untrue.' Perhaps I am digressing here, but I think it is important to recognize the extent to which pragmatism has infected our worldview and our approach to God. Pragmatism is dangerous ground for the God-follower. We do not follow God because doing so will make us healthy, wealthy, and wise, nor because it will give us better businesses or happier families. We believe in God because He is True. He is Real.

God is the Reality before, behind, and beyond all reality. He is the most real thing, the most real person. The God we find in the pages of Scripture is the One True God because *He is*, not because we find it convenient or helpful to believe Him to be. The Bible is the means He chose to capture and communicate the specific revelation of Himself to humanity. We find in the pages of Scripture the most consistent and reliable guide to the nature of God, the universe – and *everything*.

Many still do not know about Jesus Christ. Paul points out that people can learn basic things about God from observing the creation, but that they cannot come to know Him without hearing about Jesus.[155] Someone has to make the introduction.[156] Those who have tasted and seen that God is good have the privilege to share this good news with others.[157] We get to share some really good news with people who may not hear in any other way!

Many people hold incredibly damaged and damaging ideas about God. Some view Him as a malevolent genocidal tyrant, always angry and ready to judge. Ideas like this make Him terrifying and unappealing. This picture of God has much more in common with the Muslim view of God than the complete biblical picture. Why would I want a relationship with a God like that? Others have a view of God as a distant and kind figure who rarely involves Himself on earth. He bears a striking resemblance to Santa Claus, but without keeping a list of who is naughty and nice. He has no law and no standards, just a gentle, meek sort of love. This view of God also does violence to the Scriptures, deleting all those pesky passages about sin and repentance. This kind but impotent God is not worthy of respect or admiration. There is no justice in this view. Jesus warns us that He did not come to destroy the law, but to fulfill it.[158] Jesus' sinless life satisfied the needs of justice and allows us to freely enter in to a love relationship with God.

We need to be careful not to re-make God in our own image. Our various cultures pull us in different directions, but the Scriptures unite us as Christians. The only way to know what is true about God is to understand what the Bible says about Him. This understanding is the starting point for our relationship with Him, and it is the path that we continue to walk as we mature in Christ.

As I have mentioned, the church where I grew up heavily emphasized knowledge of the Scriptures. Knowledge was exalted and drilled into our heads. There were Bible memory verse competitions and 'Bible Bowls' where we were quizzed on obscure Bible trivia. The importance of knowledge was constantly emphasized. I'm grateful for the Sunday School teachers who filled my head with information, although I didn't always feel that way at the time. I recognize now that they gave me a storehouse of information – a veritable treasure trove to draw upon later in life. They also instilled in me respect for the Bible and the importance of proper interpretation. I'm not as certain as they sometimes were about one particular interpretation being the only possible one, but I appreciate their love for the Scriptures.

Paul warns us that we should be careful to rightly divide the word of truth.[159] James warns that not many of us should aspire to be teachers because teachers will incur a stricter judgment.[160] Peter and Paul both warn us about false teachers who lead others astray.[161] Clearly, we need to handle the Scriptures with care. We need to mine the jewels beneath the surface as well as pick up the many clear and explicit teachings that are in plain sight on the surface of the Scriptures.

We must not treat the Bible as a source text for whatever point we would like to prove. Some have said that the Bible can be used to prove any position. I would agree, but only if you choose to approach it with malicious intent. For example, I once came across a book claiming the Bible teaches there is no God, quoting chapter and verse. I couldn't believe it, so I looked it up. Sure enough, it's in there: Psalm 14:1 says, "There is no God." However, if you read just a bit of the context it says, "The fool says in his heart, 'There is no God.'" It was such a blatant attempt to misuse the Scriptures that I laughed aloud. Other misuses of Scripture are more subtle and less worthy of laughter, like when Satan twisted the words of God into temptations for Jesus in the wilderness.[162] My upbringing gave me a strong 'heresy monitor' and spotting heresy was like playing *Name that Tune*.[163] I can name that heresy in five sentences! We were adept at spotting deviations from the standard line and pronouncing judgment with a vengeance. However, we were so confident in our particular interpretations of virtually every passage that any divergence from the pastor's views was equated with being unbiblical, if not downright heretical. I cringe when I think of how quick I was to cry foul over issues that I now see are open to several interpretations.

It is important to differentiate between revelation and interpretation. Revelation is the thing that we are looking at and interpretation is the way in which we understand the thing itself. For example, science is the interpretation of the material universe, which is the general revelation of God. Since God created the universe, it reveals quite a bit about Him.[164] Science interprets the data available to us in the physical universe; it pokes and prods, it investigates and questions, it organizes and explains. Similarly, theology is the interpretation of the specific revelation of God. The Scriptures were created by God to reveal Himself to us with greater specificity than we would be able to obtain otherwise. Nevertheless, the Scriptures need to be studied and interpreted, and in doing so we need the help of God the Holy Spirit who guides us into all truth.[165]

A common problem in both science and theology is not distinguishing between revelation and interpretation. We often equate our interpretation with revelation. We make the mistake of saying, "Science proves this" or "The Bible says that" and therefore anyone who disagrees with us is plainly disagreeing with science or God. Disagreeing with our interpretation does not necessarily mean disagreeing with God or the Bible. This is a logical fallacy. Let me be clear: Many, many things are explicitly taught in Scripture. However, other things are less clear and, within historic orthodox faith, latitude exists in interpreting these things.

The study and interpretation of the Scriptures requires humility. I can believe that the Scriptures are inspired by God just as I believe the stars are His handiwork.[166] But that doesn't mean that I perfectly understand either the Scriptures or the stars. Understanding and interpreting are usually hard work. Just as scientists studying the same data honestly disagree about how to interpret it, theologians can honestly disagree about our interpretation of a particular passage efefefefef/ef

or an idea contained in Scripture.[167] Often, Christians are too quick to attack one another at the point where our doctrines diverge. I cannot count the number of times I have heard the accusation leveled at me – or others – that we didn't believe the Bible, when a point of interpretation was the real issue.[168] I believe the Bible is the only unchanging and reliable guide for our faith. That does not mean that my interpretation doesn't grow or mature over time. I am committed to learning for the rest of my life and this requires the admission that I don't know it all now. Christians will not always agree on our interpretations and we can and should engage in vigorous debate with one another. We should discuss our disagreements and varying interpretations, but we must do so with humility and love. We should sharpen one another, but not with sharp words.[169] We can offer each other flexibility and grace, without being so flexible that we turn the Scriptures into some sort of textual playdough that we can squeeze into any shape we desire. We must hold on to Truth. Truth is important. We must be tenacious in our hold on it, and hold loosely to our interpretation of things that are less-clear teachings of Scripture. I like the common formulation: In essentials unity, in non-essentials diversity, in all things love.[170]

Seeking God in community is an indispensable aspect of our intellectual life. To love God with our minds and think right thoughts about Him, we must not stop with just information about God; instead, we should push through to engage in relationship with God Himself. And we must do this work together! In community, we interpret Scripture with an attitude of mutual submission and humility, offering our observations and ideas to one another to be corrected or improved on by the community.

The goal of our intellectual pursuits is not just knowledge. It's relationship. The life of the mind finds its best expression in relationship with God and in supportive community. We learn how to communicate in community. We learn how to listen and express ourselves. We also learn how to recognize and resolve miscommunication and misunderstandings.

If you want to know God, I would suggest you start by reading the book He has written. If you are early in your relationship with God and are wondering where to start, I encourage you to start with one of the Gospels: Matthew, Mark, Luke, or John – the first four books of the New Testament. These record the life and teachings of Jesus. By reading about Jesus, you will get a picture of God. When you have seen Jesus, you have seen God because He is the image of God.[171] It is hard for us to imagine the Spirit who created all things. Because Jesus came to earth as a man, we get an image of God in human form, one we can relate to *and* who can relate to us.[172] The incarnation helps us connect with God and get to know Him in ways that would be more difficult otherwise.

Some people claim they want to know God, but they don't actually do anything about it. If we want to know God, He is there to be known. He promises He will draw near to us if we will draw near to Him.[173] It's not just knowledge about God that we are after; we want to know God personally. We must treat our quest like a relationship, because it is a relationship. If I want to strengthen my relationship with my wife, I will seek her out. I will try to get to know her, not just gather information about her.

As you begin to pursue God through the Scriptures, you may find that He will gently but firmly point out areas in your life that are inhibiting your relationship with Him. Some barriers to intimacy may be things that you do and you know you shouldn't do; others may be things you aren't doing even though you know you should. Still others may be brand-new things you have never thought of. I don't know where He will lead you, but I do know that if you seek you will find; if you knock, the door will be opened to you.[174]

CHAPTER 8: REFLECTION QUESTIONS

- *What place has the concept of right thinking held in your life and faith up to this point?*

- *What are you doing to develop your intellect? How can you better love God with your mind?*

- *What are some wrong thoughts or beliefs that have found expression in your life? What can you do to combat these thoughts?*

- *What are your thoughts on the difference between revelation and interpretation? Can you identify a time when you've seen a problem arise by confusing the two?*

- *How can you grow in your knowledge of God? What are some practical steps you can take?*

- *How can you engage with others to grow your knowledge of Truth?*

THE WILL
Finding our Way to Right Living

Just as God created us with intellectual capacity, He has also given us the ability to make choices. In fact, most of what gets into our minds is a result of our choices. We decide whether to read or to listen. We make a choice to attend a class or go to the movies. We choose to buy music or hang out with our friends.

All of these and a myriad of other choices, some consciously made and others not, largely determine the paths of our lives. Our lifestyles are the conglomeration of the decisions we make. We are all in the process of *becoming*. Our choices have a massive impact on what we become. How will I spend my time, my energy, my money? Which projects or relationships will I develop?

Bob was a young man who seemed to be hungry to grow. We met each week to spur one another on.[175] However, after a few weeks of meeting together, I began to wonder if Bob actually wanted to grow. He seemed to talk a good talk, but between our meetings, he would not do the readings we agreed upon, or follow through on other things in his life. I eventually asked him if he really wanted to grow, and if he was willing to do something about it. He assured me that he was ready to invest in growth. I gave him the assignment to read the book we were going through before our next meeting.

In order to provide a little extra incentive, we agreed that we would not meet again until he had completed the book.

The following week, he showed up at our normal meeting time. I was relieved, assuming this meant he had completed the reading. To confirm, I asked him if he had, and he sheepishly admitted that he had not. I was surprised. I asked him why he hadn't called to let me know, and whether we had been unclear in our agreement. He readily admitted that we had agreed not to meet until he had done the reading, but then asked if we could flex on that point. I said, "No," and told him I would be happy to meet with him as soon as he finished the book. I suggested that he give me a call whenever he was done, even if it was later that day or the following day. He asked if we could continue our regular meeting times and I declined, instead inquiring whether the book was too much to read or too difficult. As he was a university student living at home for the summer without employment, he admitted he had plenty of time. To which I responded, "Good, I look forward to meeting with you as soon as you get it done."

A few weeks later, a friend of his approached me and asked me if I was still meeting with Bob. She was eager for him to receive spiritual input to encourage his relationship with God. I told her that I shared her eagerness, explained our agreement and suggested that she ask Bob about it. She came back a few days later and reported that Bob told her we were indeed still meeting weekly, and that our next appointment would happen just as soon as he finished the book. Bob never finished the book. He never called and we never met again.

Scripture tells us we will reap what we sow.[176] All of our choices are planting seeds that will grow and bear fruit. The question is... what kind of seeds we will plant? If I sow angry words and hurtful actions, I will reap broken relationships and loneliness. If I sow seeds of drunkenness, gluttony, and debauchery, I will reap a wrecked body and leave a trail of brokenness in my wake. On the other hand, if I sow forgiveness and gentleness, I will reap trust and close relationships. If I sow into my relationship with God, I will reap intimacy and the fruit of the Spirit in my life.[177]

God invites us to bring our will under submission to His – a safe place to be since He is good and He knows all things. Scripture describes God as the Alpha and the Omega (the first and the last letters of the Greek alphabet).[178] He is before all things and in all things.[179] He knows all things and He specifically knows all the days of our life. We do not know what lies in our future, but God does.[180] I will not attempt to explain this mystery.[181] But take a moment to contemplate the implications: If God is for us and He knows all things, wouldn't it be wise to bring our choices in line with His? If God loves us and has good plans for us, wouldn't we want to be in on the plan? Bringing our will under submission to His is the wisest thing we can do!

This relational view of God shapes the way we read the commands of God in the Scriptures. Too often, when we read His commands they seem burdensome. We interpret them through the lens of our own selfish and limited perspective and see them as keeping good things from us. Like Adam and Eve in the garden, we see the thing denied as pleasing to the eye and good; we doubt the goodness of God when He denies us what we want.[182] This view of God as One Who withholds good things from us is not at all accurate. We are not left in the dark to imagine what God is like; we can make choices that will lead us to discover who God really is. These choices to intentionally pursue God are commonly called spiritual disciplines.

Keeping our relational view in mind frees us from the legalistic practice of spiritual disciplines. We do not choose to pray because it earns us points with God, or because a failure to pray will result in us being judged by Him. We pray because it is part of our relationship with God. We speak and we listen through prayer. We do not study

the Bible 'or else…' We study it because it is part of how we grow in
our relationship with God. We do not obey the commands of God
because we fear retribution – fear is a lousy long-term motivator!
We seek to bring our lives in line with the best way to live, which is
within the parameters revealed to us by our kind and loving Father,
Brother, and Counselor.

This relational view allows us to be intentional about our choices
while also protecting us from bizarre extremes or fear-motivated
duty. God's Word is a lamp to our feet and a guide to our path.[183]
He understands the structure of the universe from a perspective we
cannot even imagine. He knows what is best for our bodies, our souls,
our relationships with other people and the rest of creation. His Word
points the way to a right understanding of Him and everything else.
Obedience to God is simply smart; it is the path of wisdom and right
relationship. Remembering this serves us well when we struggle to
believe. Blaise Pascal acknowledged that it is not always easy for us
to find our way to faith. It was in the context of this difficulty that he
formulated his advice to wager on God. Essentially, Pascal said that
in a situation where there is at least as much evidence *for* as there is
against something, then we should discover which one would be more
advantageous and then live as if it was true.[184] When we do this, we
are putting ourselves in a position to find out if it is true through the
laboratory of life and experience.[185]

I have found this idea of devotional experimentation to be an
important part of my journey. My study of the Scriptures leads me
to believe that God is real and that He wants to be known. The
amazing truth that God wants to know me and be known by me is
only an abstract idea until I respond to the invitation. I must begin
to pursue Him, to reach out for Him. My reaching out for Him is
a rudimentary act of faith, or at least hope.[186]

Even if you do not now believe in God, you can begin to
investigate – to search for Him. Even if you have no faith, you can

step out in hope. You can begin to live in such a way as to discover if God is real. The wager is not the end of the journey, but the beginning of a search. Making the choice to wager on God means setting aside the things that inhibit your ability to experience Him, and doing things that will increase the likelihood of meeting Him along the way.

If I told you that I had just spotted a rare bird and invited you to come and see it, you would have some choices before you. First, am I someone you trust, or am I the kind of person that would tell you something untrue? Second, are you interested in seeing the bird for yourself? If you decide I am trustworthy and you want to see the bird, then you have more choices to make. You might decide to ask me where I spotted it. You might inquire about what kind of equipment I used, or what time of day or what weather conditions would be advantageous. You might ask if there were things you should avoid wearing or doing that might spook the bird. Based on these inquiries, you could form a plan to search for the bird and put the plan into action. I could tell you the story of how I saw the bird and share with you all my best tips on how to spot the elusive bird, but in order to actually see the bird, you would have to go and spot it yourself.

Obviously, this analogy breaks down at some point, but the general principles are applicable. The beauty of pursuing God is that He wants to be found. He is not hiding or taunting us from the underbrush. He has gone to great lengths to make Himself accessible. Those of us who have experienced Him can share about our relationship with Him; however, if you want to find Him, you will need to launch out on your own voyage of discovery. He interacts with each person differently, although His nature and character never change.

Reading the Bible and praying are among the most basic spiritual disciplines. Both are good practices that will not lead us astray, but they are not the only helpful practices available. I will end this chapter with a discussion on prayer, but first I'd like to explore other practices that can help us to discover God around us.

One practical choice is to abstain from things that pull us away from God. The Bible calls these things sin. Jeremiah sums up all of the sins of the people of Israel this way, "My people have committed two sins: They have forsaken me, the spring of living water, and have dug their own cisterns, broken cisterns that cannot hold water."[187] All our sin falls into two categories. Either we haven't gone to God when we should have (He is always ready to meet with us and care for us) or we've gone to something other than God (something that will not satisfy us and will ultimately fail us). So, we are constantly faced with two basic choices: the choice to pursue God or not, and the choice to turn away from things that compete with God for our attention and affection or not.

One of the vows I made to my wife on our wedding day was "forsaking all others, to be faithful to her as long as we both shall live." That means that I don't entertain any competitors for my romantic affections. I have given my love to my wife and I must resist all temptations or opportunities to give my love to another. This is also required in our relationship with God. Anything that draws our affections is suspect, even if morally neutral. For example, reading is not inherently evil, but if I allow reading to come between me and God, it has become a problem. But of course not all things crying for our time and attention are morally neutral. God specifically warns us to avoid things that do nothing but damage; these things are off limits to us not because we'll get in trouble, but because they are counterproductive to developing the relationship we want.

If I want my garden to grow, I don't poison the plants. Instead, I do things that will help to promote their growth. It's simply common sense: Don't poison stuff you don't want to kill. Protect stuff you want to grow. This truth is not difficult to understand, but it is often difficult to put into practice. We have already observed that we have an enemy who seeks our destruction; and we are also driven by internal motivations, which we'll explore more in the next chapter. As we actively choose growth, we learn dependence on the presence and power of God to help us follow through on our good intentions.

Assuming that you are ready to give up the bad stuff, the next step is to do positive things. Gary Thomas' *Sacred Pathways* is excellent on this subject.[188] Thomas encourages us to experience God in different ways and shows that these various ways are firmly grounded in Scripture. In the introduction, Thomas uses the analogy of visiting a doctor for an ailment. He points out that if the doctor prescribes antibiotics each time you go, regardless of your situation or your ailment, the antibiotics will not likely kill you; however, they might not be the best treatment option either. He compares this to the stock answer for many people struggling spiritually – to read the Bible and pray. This will never kill you as a Christian, but there are a variety of avenues available to us for the cultivation of a more intimate relationship with God.

Henri Nouwen's short book, *The Way of the Heart*, is also invaluable.[189] Nouwen encourages the disciplines of solitude and silence as foundational practices for those who would draw near to God. I was first given this book many years ago by a mentor. At the time, I was going through a dry and difficult period in my relationship with God. I was reading the Bible and praying, I was attending church, but I still felt distant. Solitude and silence have since become an indispensible part of my journey.

Another key discipline is to seek out and develop real community.[190] Real community means living life with people – letting them into my life and engaging with them in theirs. As mentioned earlier, this requires a vulnerability and trust that is best cultivated over time. As we choose to remove our masks with at

least a few close friends, we learn to live from who we actually are
and become who we can be – the one Christ will recreate us to be.

I mention these practices not because I'm prescribing the same
specific practices for you. My goal is to describe some of what has
been helpful for me personally, and encourage you to find practices
that are helpful for you. (See the appendices for resources and
suggestions.) Solitude is never a bad thing, but it may not be the
best practice for you at this time. It's not a question of whether or
not we should be intentionally engaged in spiritual disciplines; it is a
question of which ones to focus on at different stages in our journey
and relationship with God.

We have a wonderful Partner in this process. God the Holy
Spirit wants to guide and direct us in the paths that will help us to
grow closer to Him.[191] We don't need to fret about which practices
or lifestyle changes we need to make, but we do need to start
somewhere. This is where community really helps. Having people
we can talk to about our journey opens up new avenues for growth,
an infusion of new ideas and options. Often, others will have walked
our portion of the journey before. They can ask good questions or
share their own experiences, perhaps pointing us in directions we
had not considered, like my friend who gave me the Nouwen book.
Our first choice must be to actually do something.

Imagine a man who wants to learn how to ride a bicycle. He reads
books about bicycling. He subscribes to bicycling magazines. He talks
to an expert cyclist. He talks with his friends about biking. He takes
classes on the history of cycling. While some of these things might
actually help, the one thing that surely will help is to actually get on
a bike and start pedaling. As he starts to pedal, he will learn along
the way. He may want to take a class, or read about how to improve a
particular technique, but nothing can replace the experience of riding.

The Chesterton quote from chapter two comes to mind again:
"The Christian ideal has not been tried and found wanting, it has

been found difficult and left untried." We must actually try. A good place to start is prayer. Prayer is already a step of engagement with God. Choosing to tell God about my frustrations with Him is a very biblical kind of prayer; we find many examples of this throughout the Scriptures. It is ironic that we often seek people out to discuss our difficulties with God but don't talk with God about it directly. Lament is an important part of our life with God. So is praise and worship. They are all part of our repertoire of prayer.

Communication is the cornerstone of any relationship. It is particularly important when there are difficulties and doubts. It is good to talk with God about our doubts. Doubt is not the opposite of faith; it is *apathy* that stands opposed to faith and relationship. God wants us to unmask ourselves with Him and not just tell Him what we think He wants to hear. He is not impressed with theological treatises in our prayers. His theology is already better and purer than ours. Our prayers should be about asking, seeking, knocking, listening, and receiving.

Michael Card, in his book *Sacred Sorrow*, points out that this is the key difference between Job and Job's friends.[192] The Old Testament book of Job is a story about incredible suffering and the silence of God. Essentially, Job loses everything and begins to lament. He pours out his heart to God and even blasts God with accusations. His friends step in and correct his theology. Job responds by engaging in a prolonged debate with his friends about whether God is good and who is to blame. Toward the end of the book, God steps in and reinitiates the direct conversation with Job. The next few chapters are again a dialogue between God and Job. The surprise conclusion to the book is that God asks Job to pray for his friends. Job, the one who argued with God, is not the one with whom God is angry. God is angry with the friends who tried to defend Him from Job![193] God asks Job to pray for them.[194] Throughout the book, Job's friends never talked with God, only about Him, accusing Job and misrepresenting God in the process. In contrast, Job's perspective was realigned and corrected as he engaged with God directly.

Job's story brings to mind the biblical account of God changing Jacob's name.[195] Jacob argues and wrestles with God all night. In the end, he receives a new name: Israel. Israel means 'contends or struggles with God.' I love that the followers of God are called the sons of Israel. According to Paul, we have been grafted into Israel.[196] The name of the family of God is 'those who wrestle with God.' We are supposed to grapple with Him.

We start from this place of intentionally entering into prayer, even when it feels like our prayers barely make it off the ground or simply bounce off the ceiling. We choose to wrestle with God. We choose to live as if it is true and then we discover the reality of it in the doing.

Recently, I was working with a man who said he had never seen or experienced God. After talking for a while, I encouraged him to start a prayer journal. He looked at me rather skeptically, but agreed to pray each evening before going to sleep and to write down at least one thing that He asked God for. The following week, he came in with a broad smile and shared how excited he was that he had seen God answer several specific prayers in just one week. His excitement wasn't merely about the concrete answers; it was about the fact that he was now talking *with* God rather than just talking *about* God. I could have given him a book on prayer or told him my own experiences of God, but nothing could replace his personal experience of meeting with God in his own life.

The individual choice to renew our minds and to offer ourselves to the Lord renews us day by day.[197] This is worship, the choice to offer ourselves.[198] The choice to pursue Him and to forsake the other things that call for our attention and affection is a pure act of worship.

As we intentionally choose to cultivate new ways of living, our relationship with God will grow. We will find our lifestyle changing as we engage with the living God. We are meant for more than just a set of outward behaviors shaped by our will. Our journey toward intimacy necessarily involves the will, but a real relationship engages the emotions as well, as we will examine in the next chapter.

CHAPTER 9: REFLECTION QUESTIONS

- *Have you found the pursuit of God difficult and left it untried, as G.K. Chesterton suggests many have?*

- *How good are you at making decisions and following through?*

- *Are you choosing to pray and to seek God through His Word? Are you journaling? Are you practicing solitude or silence? Are you choosing community?*

- *What spiritual disciplines have you practiced? Are there disciplines you have not practiced but feel you should?*

- *What are some choices you can make (perhaps lifestyle choices) that will move you forward in your relationship with God?*

THE EMOTIONS
Finding Emotional Healing

Do you ever have a hard time believing something? I know I do. Do you ever have a hard time consistently living out the things you believe? I do, too.

For example, I have a hard time believing that God is entirely trustworthy. Intellectually, I know this to be true, because it is clearly taught in Scripture.[199] But there seems to be quite a distance between my head, my heart, and my hands on this one. I see His faithfulness in the pages of Scripture. I read about His faithfulness in the lives of others. I can preach and testify about His faithfulness in my own life; but to consistently live from that place of belief is hard.

My life and my choices often reveal a contradiction. Although I trust God, I still try to make sure that I will be safe and secure in the event that God doesn't come through for me. I'm hesitant to venture out into the unknown where God's faithfulness would be my only hope for success. I'm farther along on my journey of belief than ever before, but still I struggle. This struggle demonstrates the distance between my intellectual assent and core emotional beliefs.

For centuries, we in the West have been moving away from our emotions. We have separated our intellect from our emotions and have highly valued information and logic while denigrating our emotional capacity. We have adopted a Greek (Western) approach to knowledge over a Hebraic (Eastern) one. For the Greek and Roman, knowledge was information to be debated and understood intellectually. Knowing was an intellectual exercise. For the ancient Hebrews, knowledge was expressed as wisdom – information put into practice in life. Until something was lived and experienced, it was not truly known.

I met Sam at a conference. He had been in full-time ministry for many years. He seemed to be a good guy, confident and competent. He asked if we could grab a cup of coffee. As we sat down with Starbucks in hand, he told me how he felt hindered in his marriage and his relationship with God. I was humbled by his trust and surprised that he invited me so deeply into his journey. As I asked more questions and listened carefully to his responses, I was relieved to find he was coming to me not in brokenness because he had acted out in some way, but rather because he recognized the danger and was eager for help. All too often, people don't ask for help until after they have made a tragic mistake.

Over the next few days, we met several times. I continued to ask questions to help him to discover the source, or sources, of the barrier he was feeling. It became clear that there was some sort of block to intimacy for him. I knew the context in which he lived and worked and suspected there might be a spiritual source behind this. I drew a very bad rendition of *The Five Circles* on a napkin, carefully explaining how each area interconnected. He asked a number of clarifying questions. Once I was confident he understood the model, I asked him if he would be willing to think and pray about identifying an area to focus on. He agreed.

The next day when we met, he seemed confident that the emotional area was where he needed to focus. I was surprised and asked a few more questions to probe the spiritual area, as I had been fairly certain that this was a major factor. As we talked, he said he felt God was calling him to probe the area of past hurts, particularly his family of origin. Over the next few months, it became clear that this was the right decision. As he began to intentionally explore that part of his life, some progress was made, but he still felt stuck.

More than a year after our first meeting, we found ourselves attending another conference together. We scheduled a time to meet for prayer. I facilitated the prayer time and encouraged Sam to focus on listening for God's voice and being attentive to any impressions or images. Neither of us knew what to expect; we just knew that we were inviting God to speak to Sam and to guide him toward freedom. Over the next hour, God brought several very painful memories to Sam's mind, some of which he had not consciously revisited for many years. Then, God did the most amazing thing: He showed Sam where He was in the scenes from his childhood. Perhaps even more amazing was that God showed me several of the same scenes from Sam's life. Since I had not been part of his life in those early years, they were things I could not have remembered – or known anything about.

Sam was moved to tears as he experienced God's tender care for him as never before. His knowledge of God's love moved beyond intellect to emotion that day; it became real and very personal. The damaging formative experiences that had prevented him from making himself vulnerable, a necessary precursor to true intimacy, were reformed by God's revelation of Himself. God gave Sam a new formative experience of His love as a part of His continuing work to make him new.

Both the intellectual and emotional parts of us are made in the image of God. He is brilliant; He has a full and robust intellectual life. He also has a full and robust emotional life. God experiences and expresses a full range of emotions in Scripture. He loves. He grieves. He weeps. He gets angry. He hates. He rejoices. He is fully-orbed emotionally.[200] He has unbounded emotional capacity within the community of the Godhead and expresses this toward humanity. Our God is relational and emotional; and He made us in His image.

Growing closer to God cannot only involve the spirit, intellect and will. It also requires an emotional and relational pursuit. To ignore any component of ourselves is dangerous. The modernist danger was to develop the body, the intellect, and the will while neglecting the emotions and the spirit. We saw this played out in the great destruction of the 20th Century. The postmodernist danger is to neglect the intellect for the emotions. There is a ditch on either side of the road. We avoid the ditches by holding a robust and biblical view of God and of ourselves. We cannot just select the aspects we find most appealing or easiest to understand. We must develop all of who we are to become who God wants us to be. The intellect is an essential part of knowing God; it provides the information we need to fall in love with Him. As we act on this information, our relationship develops beyond mere information and becomes a life of love – a life of worship expressed from our hearts.

Our intellectual statements about God are much less important than what we actually *believe*. Our true beliefs about God are often obscured by our religious words and practices.[201] On an emotional level, we never act contrary to what we truly believe. When we act contrary to what we *say* we believe, we unwittingly reveal our lack of true heart-level belief. This is why the Scriptures tell us that from the heart flow the issues of life.[202] Jesus said that it is not what goes into a man that makes him unclean, but rather the words and actions that come out of a man reveal the uncleanness within.[203] We cannot neglect the heart, for it reveals the true state of our beliefs.

When I talk about the emotional part of our humanness, I mean the source of our feelings and truly deep beliefs. In the West, we often talk about this as the heart, but I'm not sure we are always clear on what we mean. Our emotions are a critical part of our multifaceted relational capacity. They are the parts of us that love and fear, that trust and doubt; and this is a key component of our being made in the image of God. We can relate to people and to God sympathetically and emotionally because of this part of who we are.

Jesus said that the first and greatest commandment is to love God.[204] This is not an act of the intellect or will alone – these would be insufficient. Loving God must include the emotions. Of course it involves the mind and the will, but these alone would be insufficient. God wants more than just intellectual assent to His reality. He wants more than just the exercise of the will to bring our behavior into line with the way the universe really works. God wants a relationship with us.

In order to love God more completely, we must expand our emotional capacity. The emotional part of ourselves can grow and be developed just as our bodies and our minds can. We can also be wounded or stunted emotionally. Each one of us has been damaged at some point. We simply do not feel as we should. As we begin to grow and heal in this emotional part of ourselves, we may feel more and more that this world is not as it should be. We may feel that something is wrong and warped. We were not made for death or hate. We were not made for lies and abuse. We were made for a true world, a paradise without lies, death, or pain. We were made for heaven on earth.[205] But none of us were raised in heaven. No one since the fall of Adam and Eve has experienced this world as it was meant to be experienced. We have all tasted the bitter disappointment of living in a broken world, with broken families, broken communities, and broken hearts. We were not made for this.

But life on Earth is all we know for the time being, and so we learn to protect ourselves. We learn to make the best of a bad situation. We wall-off or shut down portions of our emotions because it is simply too painful to be truehearted in a false world. However, as we grow we find that the walls we originally built to protect ourselves now prevent us from being who we were made to be. Although they may have served us well at one point, now they constrict us, even strangle us. We must break down these walls or remain stunted. We cannot hide behind our defenses and truly experience the freedom, grace, and love of God. We must have the courage to surrender to His love, the love that casts out all fear.[206] We must explore our feelings and engage our emotions again. This may feel dangerous to us, perhaps like disarming in the middle of a war. After all, we continue to live in a broken world.

God meets us exactly at this point of need. We have a God who knows what we are going through. Jesus lived in this broken world. He was despised and rejected.[207] He was misunderstood and mistreated. We have a God who sympathizes with us and who meets us on the road. God knows emotional torment. He knows us intimately, and can provide healing and protection for our hearts.

Often this healing will come through members of His family, the community of God. Growing in our relationship with God cannot be divorced from growing in our relationship with people. Our emotional capacity toward God and people emanates from the same part of ourselves. To wall ourselves off from people is to remain walled off from God. To open ourselves to God will mean opening ourselves to people. John clarifies that we cannot hate God's people and still claim to love God.[208]

Sometimes God will choose to heal us directly. The healing we receive from God will then overflow into the lives of those around us; we are more capable of giving and receiving love and comfort because we have received it.[209] Often the healing will come through the medium of people, but this involves risk because no one is perfect in this life.

The degree to which we are secure in our identity in God is the degree to which we can overcome our fear and forgive others. As we receive healing, we move toward ever-increasing freedom. To the degree that we cannot forgive, neither can we receive forgiveness. We are perfectly forgiven by God because of the work of Christ. That is an established fact. However, we cannot receive that fact as real for us until we experience it. The fullness of this experience is found in forgiving others and being forgiven by them.[210]

Jesus promised that anyone who was thirsty could come to Him and drink. He promised that if we did, the Holy Spirit would well up within us.[211] This is real! This can be experienced! It's not a physical welling up; intimacy with God can and should be experienced in the emotional part of who we are. This may sound strange, but it shouldn't. We experience feelings of love and closeness with other human beings, and this should point us toward an even deeper kind of intimacy that is available to us. Human love is amazing, even though it is but a dim reflection of divine love. Western cultures have elevated romantic love to the pinnacle of human experience. Don't get me wrong. As a recipient of amazing love from my parents, my wife, and my children, I get the attraction. Human love is tremendous! Nevertheless, human love is a light bulb compared to the sun of God's love. We have substituted the reflection for the real thing and we deny the possibility of the divine. To a man living in darkness the light bulb is an incredible gift, a thing of beauty; but we were made for the sun! We were made to bask in the glorious radiance of the divine sun of righteousness.[212]

We cannot get there without receiving healing. All of us have been wounded in some way. Some of us have suffered horrifically damaging abuse. Even those of us who have lived relatively sheltered lives will need to unlearn patterns of feeling and relating that limit our ability to experience intimacy with God and people. It may be difficult to begin exploring our feelings. For many of us it will involve a plunge into uncharted depths, and we may fear the dark shadows lurking beneath the surface. We need someone to walk alongside us. We don't do this alone. We do this in community, even if not everyone in our communities will be safe. Perhaps no one in our current community is safe, but we can't let this stop us.

I don't know anyone who has been around the Church for any length of time who has not been wounded by people in the Church. We need community if we are to grow and heal emotionally. Therefore, we must work to build healing communities, communities of transformation, where it is safe to dismantle our defenses. It is unrealistic to think this will happen in large groups. We must form small communities within the Body of Christ where trust can be cultivated and real soul friendships can emerge. Community is not easy, but neither is it optional. When we come into relationship with God, we become part of the Family of God. We can serve by loving each other well as we grow in an atmosphere of humility and mutual commitment.

One of the ways that God heals us from previous relationships is through current relationships. Within the relative safety of the caring community of Christ, God re-trains our emotions.[213] If we begin to tear down the walls of self-protection and find that we are loved instead of attacked, we will find the courage to tear down more sections of our defenses. Then we will find new sweetness in our relationships with others and an expanding capacity to experience God.

Choosing to become part of a real community is a move toward healing. We learn to feel rightly as we experience healthy, life-giving relationships. As we begin to heal, we have more capacity for healthy relating and this begets a virtuous cycle of healing and growth. As we begin to give and receive forgiveness and love, we grow in our capacity to do so.

Our healing will have other consequences as well. We will find that our coping mechanisms become uncomfortable or simply fall away. We will no longer be driven to escape from our feelings, our lives, or ourselves. As our false selves and self-destructive patterns are overcome, cast aside, or fade away, we find fewer hindrances in our relationship with God and with others.

Being a part of real community is always good, but sometimes our healing may require more intentional treatment. Sometimes this will take the form of counseling. Counseling was a key part of my own journey toward intimacy with God. It provided a safe environment to express and explore the wounds of my past. I found as I did so, I was no longer driven in the same way to run to things I had used to self-medicate. I was, and still am, tempted to return to the cisterns of my youth; however, I am no longer *compelled* as I once was. Year by year, as the healing continues, I find my capacity to be satisfied in God increasing. I also find an increasing capacity to rightly take pleasure in the things He gives me to enjoy, as these reflected pleasures no longer replace the one true Treasure.

As we saw in Sam's story, another means for healing is prayer.[214] There are a number of schools of thought and practice such as inner healing, healing of memories, or wholeness prayer.[215] While many practitioners of these methods would make much about the differences between them, for the purposes of this discussion, we will focus on the similarities. In general, these models invite God to meet with the person in need of healing directly in and through prayer.

I won't take the time here to explain each of these practices, but I have included information in the resource section at the end of the book for those who are interested. What I will focus on is the fact that all of these models create avenues for the person to come directly into contact with God. He knows exactly where the source of the difficulty lies. He also knows which symbols or words will speak to the heart of the person in need. I have seen remarkable breakthroughs in a very short time as God addresses things directly through these methods. One caveat with this model is that the minister cannot promise results.[216] The person who is facilitating the session helps create the environment for God to speak but cannot compel God to speak or the needy person to hear. There is no room for blame in this model. Sometimes healing happens and sometimes not. We have to allow for the mystery of God's interactions with each person to remain.

There is mystery in all communication; however, we cannot use the reality of this mystery as an excuse to not engage. Instead, we choose to seek intimacy and to bear the difficulties inherent in the task. As I seek to help people to grow in their relationship with God, I need to allow their relationship to be theirs alone. I cannot insert myself into it, or project my experiences upon it.

Seeking emotional healing and wholeness is not an optional part of the Christian journey. God wants us to love Him with all we are, including our emotions. If we remain disengaged and distant from God and people emotionally, we fail in the greatest commandment to love God with all we are.[217] This is a command, not a suggestion. I find it interesting that God would choose to command this, when it is obviously in our best interest. Perhaps it is because He knows how hard it is for us to love and trust. Loving God with all we are is not a peripheral issue, it is central, even though it is humanly impossible. No one ever loves God completely on this side of heaven.[218] This command once again shows us our entire dependence on our Trinitarian God. We are always thrown back on our need for Christ. He is the only human who loved God perfectly. Through His perfect life, death, resurrection, and ascension, He made a way for us to approach Father God.[219] Even though we daily fail to love God and each other with a complete and undivided heart, His grace covers us. We can boldly approach our Father on His Throne of Grace. We can live under the guidance and empowerment of the Spirit. We can keep in step with Him.[220] We can grow in our ability to connect with God. We can continue to press on. It gets easier and sweeter, even as our longing for paradise lost remains.

Christ's life, death, and resurrection are the anchor for our faith and our relationship with God. We have a God who understands our emotions because He has lived on this earth as well. The incarnation makes Christ our emotional touchstone and also roots our faith in the earthy soil of history. God did not just speak through prophets or deliver a philosophical system from afar; He lived in a physical body in our material world, just as we do.

CHAPTER 10: REFLECTION QUESTIONS

- *How comfortable are you with learning to love God with your emotions? Is this an area where you have a lot of experience? If so, what experiences have you had? If not, what practices might you consider in order to grow in this area?*

- *How has your emotional development affected other areas of your life?*

- *Can you be completely honest with God? Do you have a friend, or a small group, with whom you can be completely yourself, unmasked?*

- *How has God used community to help you grow emotionally?*

- *Have you ever practiced inner healing, wholeness prayer, or something similar?*

THE BODY
The Physical Aspect of our Journey

It may seem like a waste of time and effort to devote a chapter to our physical bodies, as one of the most obvious things about us is that we are physical beings. However, the fact that our physicality is integrally involved with our relationship with God may be less obvious.[221]

Don and I started meeting because of difficulties in his marriage. As we got to know one another, it became clear that while he came to me for help in his marriage, the issues were deeper. As our trust grew, he confessed his sexual addiction. No matter what he tried, he could not stop acting out sexually. He genuinely loved his wife, but was compulsively unfaithful to her. He was seeking help and had even submitted to a brain scan. According to Don, the scan revealed that he had effectively rewired his brain through years of sexual indulgence.[222] The damage could be undone, but it would take significant time and energy to retrain his brain.

Don's case was the first time I remember meeting with someone where the physical was such a clear and documented part of the problem. At the time (over ten years ago), my worldview simply didn't include the possibility of someone being biologically hampered in their pursuit of holiness. Since that time a lot of research has been done and brain scans have become more detailed and more common.

Today, science has more thoroughly explored the connection between our brains and our emotional and even spiritual experiences.[223]

Although Don had tried various approaches to deal with his problem on a behavioral/volitional level, nothing had worked. He tried to stop many times but felt compelled to continue his destructive behavior. Knowing what I know now, I am confident that there was a significant biological component to Don's compulsions. I encouraged Don to attack the problem from every angle. I talked to him about the long, hard road to recovery and a multi-faceted approach. I explained that he needed to get things right with God and learn how to draw near to Him to find strength and companionship for the journey. We also talked about the need for him to get counseling from a professional to help him uncover the internal emotional drivers. That was where he started to protest.

Don was willing to meet with me. He was willing to take medication. He was willing to submit to an accountability and support group; but he was unwilling to probe his past and seek help on an emotional level. He protested that he was fine – even though he clearly was not. He challenged me to tell him what was wrong with his family of origin. When I admitted I had no ideas on that front, he again asserted that he was fine. We met together a few more times. We talked about the potential spiritual element because of all the doors his behavior had opened, but again he was resistant. Eventually it became clear that he was not willing to explore any options others than the ones that were failing him. He stopped meeting with me. His behaviors continued and worsened, eventually leading to the end of his marriage.

Historically, humanity has fallen into one extreme or the other related to the body. Either we have seen the body as evil (or at least irrelevant), or we have tended to worship it.[224] It is important for us to understand God's perspective on our bodies and how our bodies relate to our pursuit of Him. After all, He created us for relationship with

Him and our design is fit for that purpose. We need to adopt God's perspective on our bodies and to honor our bodies as His beautiful creation, even as His temple.[225]

Scripture clearly teaches that God created the physical universe. Toward the end of that process, He made humans. The Genesis account says that He created us out of the dust of the earth and He breathed into us the breath of life.[226] We were created to live on the earth; we were created from the earth. We are an integral part of the physical creation. We are part material and partly immaterial. We are both physical and spiritual. When God created us in this way, He said that it was "very good."[227] In those first days, humans walked and talked with God in the paradise that was the Garden of Eden. Physical bodies were not a barrier or a hindrance to fellowship with God. Adam and Eve, the first man and woman, communed with God while inhabiting their physical bodies. Unfortunately, this didn't last long.

God gave them just one command and they broke it.[228] In doing so, sin entered the world and neither our bodies nor our souls have been the same since. We marred the image of God in us. The consequences of sin continue to impact the world today.

Nevertheless, our human bodies did not become evil. The miracle of the incarnation proves this fact. Jesus, the God-man, was born of a woman – carried inside her human body for nine months as His physical body was knit together in her womb. He went on to live a sinless life in His body. He experienced the temptations and limitations of humanity, including our physicality, all without sin. The incarnation proves that the human body is still good, despite its diminished state caused when sin entered our world.

Paul refers to our bodies as temples – the physical place where we meet with God, inhabited by God's Spirit.[229] This statement comes in a passage on sexual immorality. Paul is pointing out that it matters what we do in and with our bodies. In Romans, he picks up a similar theme when he encourages us not to use the members of our bodies for sinful purposes but instead to offer our bodies to God.[230]

The resurrection also speaks to the importance of our physicality. Scripture clearly teaches that Jesus' physical body was resurrected and that all Christians will be resurrected in the end.[231] We do not end up floating around as disembodied spirits. We will have bodies even in the next life.[232] It appears our bodies will have some different capacities or capabilities; but that we will have bodies is not in doubt. Apparently, physicality is an important part of our being in this life and the life to come. Scripture does not teach that our bodies are evil or tangential to our being. We are not *trapped* in our physical bodies; we *are* our bodies – and more.

We need to embrace our bodies as gifts from God. This perspective encourages us to take good care of them. We can make good choices about our diet, our sleep patterns, our physical disciplines, not because we 'should' but because doing so puts us in the best possible position to experience God and the world from the most healthy perspective.

Alternatively, when we are not denigrating the body, we tend to make too much of it. Our generation tends toward the exaltation of all things material, including the body. Ironically, in our efforts to exalt the human body and place it at the center of our understanding of ourselves, we have reduced our understanding of humanity to only our bodies. We have managed to lower ourselves from the pinnacle of God's creation, the only thing in all of God's creation made in Their image, to a merely physical being, a collection of chemicals and cellular structures. We have reduced ourselves to the status of a highly functioning animal – an animal at the top of the food chain, but an animal nonetheless. This strictly physical understanding of ourselves causes us to deny, or at the very least neglect, other parts of our humanity. Our approach to medicine is one area where we see this disconnect. Doctors and medical scientists have become the priests of our new faith, with a new creed, 'in medicine we trust,' not only to cure our bodies, but also to fix our souls.

From time immemorial, man has used chemicals to alter his moods and consciousness. However, it is only in the past few decades that we have seen the widespread use of medicine to treat our emotions. The treatment of the soul was long the purview of spiritual leaders. With the development of modern psychotherapy (literally 'soul treatment'), it began to move from a God-oriented process to a secular one. Even then, however, the goal was to understand the soulful aspects of ourselves, our deep motivations and desires. The general approach was to create a safe space for deep discussion and introspection in the presence of a trusted guide. In the last few years, we have moved toward a dependence on medication. It seems that we are moving away from treating our souls and toward treating our bodies as if our souls didn't exist. We treat fear, depression, or sadness as if they are merely physical maladies with a chemical cure. Rather than probing our souls, we take a pill for our bodies. We have tacitly accepted the underlying idea that our emotions and beliefs are merely manifestations of our biochemistry. Therefore, if we can change the chemical reactions we can rid ourselves of the internal discomfort.

I'm not suggesting that drugs are of no value or that our biochemistry is unimportant. On the contrary, I am sure that our biochemistry plays a significant role for some of us. However, I would suggest that not all of our emotional or relational problems can be solved with a pill. I'm concerned that the pendulum has swung too far. I am not suggesting that we should stop using anti-depressants, anti-anxiety, or other kinds of medicines available today, but I am concerned about the over-reliance upon drugs that serves to mask symptoms rather than facilitate a cure. Our souls can be cured through a holistic approach to all five aspects of humanity, including the body, rather than settling for managing the symptoms with pills.

In his book, *Brave New World*, Aldous Huxley painted a frightening picture of an imagined future. In that world, people routinely took a drug called Soma and preferred not to think, but rather to amuse themselves with entertainment, largely sensual in nature. At the time the book was written, in the early 1930s, the picture he painted was viewed as wildly imaginative, and certain aspects clearly were. However, as I look around us today, I am concerned that we have drifted perilously close to the Soma society with pills and entertainment replacing the search for true satisfaction and peace for our souls.

I am not a Luddite. I am not suggesting we should fail to avail ourselves of the aids that technology and medicine provide today, any more than we should flee from all forms of entertainment. These things can be useful if they are part of a holistic approach to life and are specifically integrated into our pursuit of God. It is when these medicines and technologies inhibit our pursuit of God that they become problematic. For example, the average American watches 2.8 hours per day of television, not including other entertainment-related activities. Imagine if we spent one less hour a day on television and intentionally used it to pursue God instead.[233]

I am not saying that I am against TV; and neither am I opposed to medicine. There are clearly times when our biochemistry affects our emotions to the point where we cannot function. Prescription drugs can help us to re-establish the equilibrium we need, so that we are better able to address the underlying issues of the soul. Sometimes the source of our discomfort *is* rooted in our biochemistry, and when treated effectively we find complete relief; but for many of us the root cause will be elsewhere and the use of drugs can help to create the space we need to deal with the root of the problem.

I have known Joy for more than a decade. She is one of those people who seems to have it all together. Joy is an incredibly gifted woman who has been an effective minister to others for many years.

A few years ago, she had the opportunity to be a part of a uniquely loving community. Among those people, she felt safer than ever before. But in that safe community a strange thing happened: long-suppressed feelings and hurts began to surface. As this happened, she began to lose her emotional equilibrium. She started to be overcome by anxiety, so much so that her ability to function in life and ministry was affected. Joy is an experienced practitioner of spiritual warfare. She also knows the Bible and she had no known areas of unrepentant sin. She was taking good care of herself physically, but the anxiety continued to grow. Joy decided to reach out for help before things got out of hand. She started seeing a counselor and taking medicine to help as she probed some tender places in her personal history. As she explored the painful areas, her sleep was affected, which further affected her ability to function. She began to take even heavier medications to help her to sleep at night and to treat her anxiety and depression during the day.

Joy came to spend some time with us on the way to an intensive residential program. What she needed from us was just friendship and love. She needed to know that she was loved and accepted even when she wasn't producing or accomplishing anything. She also needed the help she would receive in the counseling program. At the program, she bravely dove deep into her past and the trauma behind her pain. After several weeks of intense therapy, she was able to begin to reduce her medications and had recovered enough to leave the program and resume her life and ministry. Is she finished with the healing process? No. Is she off her medications? Not all of them. Joy is making use of all the available aids to move toward healing and wholeness. She is seeking wholeness for her entire person, not just one aspect. She is on the right track.

Our bodies are not all we are; they are *a part* of who we are, and as such they are necessarily involved in our lives. God created our bodies and knows how they work. Even a cursory look at the Law in the Old Testament, reveals God's concern with the way that we treat our bodies and how we use them. The body can be used for either good or evil.

In the New Testament, Paul tells us that it is good to train our bodies.[234] The body is the temple of God. We should take good care of it and use it to glorify God.[235] Paul uses physical training as an analogy for the seriousness with which we should train ourselves in godliness.[236] However, he also offers a corrective for those who would place too much emphasis on the physical. He says that physical training is of some value, but that training in godliness is of great value for both this life and our eternal life to come.[237]

Today, we take the training of the physical body seriously. In 2010, health clubs in America alone took in more than $20 billion in revenue.[238] This amount does not include the billions of dollars spent on sports equipment or workout plans aside from gym membership. The average American spends more than an hour a day on sports or exercise.[239] How we invest our time and money is an expression of what we value. We clearly value physical fitness. That's great! Our bodies are an important part of us; but I wonder what would happen if we took the fitness of our souls as seriously as the fitness of our bodies. What if we invested a little less time on our bodies and a little more time on our relationship with God?

On the other hand, many of us neglect, ignore, or even abuse our bodies and assume that it doesn't matter – that it doesn't influence our relationship with God. Every part of our lives has an influence on every other part. We are integrated beings; God made us that way. When we neglect our bodies' health, it affects our relationships, and this includes our relationship with God.

For example, early in our marriage my wife and I discovered that we often had arguments when one of us was tired or hungry. Our blood sugar and energy levels were impacted by eating and sleeping. When we ate in a regular and healthy manner, we felt better and got along better. When we got enough sleep, we saw similar results. These are commonsense things. When we make healthy choices for our body, we feel better and are freed up to interact with people (and God) from that place of health, not hindered by our self-inflicted physical maladies.

I don't like to sleep. It may sound strange, but I feel I'm missing something when I sleep. As a result, I often stay up late and don't get enough rest. When I am tired, it affects my perspective on things – I get cranky and those around me can tell the difference. Lack of sleep makes it harder to listen, read, think, focus, write, or pray. Simply choosing to take care of my body by getting enough rest helps me to see the world more accurately and to interact with people, including God, from a better place.

We must do all we can to take care of our bodies in our pursuit of God. On the other hand, we must not think that we can only experience God in a state of optimal health. Throughout history, and the pages of Scripture, we find God using physical suffering and deprivation as means to draw us to Himself. These are tools He uses in our lives, not ones that we inflict on ourselves or others.[240] If God chooses to use physical illness and suffering on our journey, we can find Him in the midst of it; but our responsibility is to love Him with all we are, including our bodies.

We cannot ignore our physical bodies and pursue God with all we are, any more than we can ignore our emotions. Neither should we overreact and make our lives all about our bodies. We need to glorify God with all of ourselves, all of our lives. Paul says it this way, "So whether you eat or drink or whatever you do, do it all for the glory of God."[241]

CHAPTER 11: REFLECTION QUESTIONS

- *How might a failure to take good care of your body negatively impact your relationship with God and others?*

- *Are you taking good care of your body (sleep, diet, exercise)? If not, what do you need to change?*

- *How well are you loving God with your body? What can you do to honor God with your body?*

- *Have you found yourself struggling to overcome soul (mental, emotional, volitional) problems without considering the physical dimension? What steps can you take to explore this area?*

- *Have you been out of balance regarding your body? Neglecting it? Over-emphasizing it? What can you do to restore a healthy balance?*

Conclusion

God invites us into a radically realigning relationship with Himself. He chose to create us and to reveal Himself to us. This revelation of Himself actually started before the creation of the first human. He showed forth His power and wisdom in creation before there was a single person outside His Trinitarian Self to appreciate it. Before the foundation of the world, God *is*, and God is *community*. Our God is One and Three; the One true God of the Bible is not a singularity but a plurality. This is the mystery of the Tri-unity, the Trinity.

God is, by definition, always relating. Behind everything that exists is an eternal, divine community. God is not a force, but a unity of persons. God the Father, the Son, and the Holy Spirit are each personalities with emotions, will, intellect, etc. Together, They are the one true God. They have eternally existed in intimate communion with one another. They are the same substance, yet distinct in personality.

God created humans in Their image. When They created the first human, They invited us into fellowship with Them. As creatures made in the image of God, humans also are inherently relational because we were made to relate to God. Our capacities are best expressed in and through relationships. We were designed with eternal relationship in mind. We were imbued with an incredible capacity for love and unbroken relationship with God and one another. Scripture speaks of our time living and working in relationship with God and one another in paradise.[242] We were given freedom to explore the world that points to Him – to walk and talk with Him in the paradise of His creation. Unfortunately, we spoiled paradise. Ever since, we live in a world of compounding unintended consequences. We were made for perfect, never-ending relationships; but we live in a broken world – a world where death destroys even the strongest of human relationships.

We were designed with the capacity for community, but we are born into a damaged world – a world where we experience isolation and separateness from birth. Many of us have been neglected by those who should have nurtured, preyed upon by those who should have protected. No matter what our family background, we have all experienced this brokenness, although not necessarily to the same degree. Through these and other experiences, we become isolated from one another. In extreme cases, we lose the ability to connect with others at all. Even the less wounded of us have been damaged in some way. We have all had our relational capacity stunted. We are broken, but not beyond repair.

The life, death, resurrection, and ascension of Jesus Christ forged a new beginning. God is making all things new, and we get to be a part of that. God is making us new.

The Five Circles is one way to represent the core aspects of our humanity. All five of these facets of ourselves influence how we relate to others, including God. Some have suggested adding a sixth circle to represent community, but I believe community is not a part of who we are; it is what we do. We relate to others. Community is what we were designed for. All five circles are facets of our relational capacity.

These Five Circles of our being are inextricably linked. We cannot disentangle them. We were never meant to treat them in isolation. We were meant to use all of our faculties and capacities together to connect with God and each other. All of the Law and the Prophets can be summed up in loving God with all we are and loving people as ourselves.[243] As we understand *The Five Circles*, they become a practical guide to aid us in identifying potential growth areas. *The Five Circles* can help us to recognize what is happening in us as well as around us. Keeping this paradigm in mind helps us to cultivate attentiveness – to ourselves, to God, to others, and to the spiritual world.

I met Mark at a conference. He shared some of his struggles with the group, and I was drawn to him. The struggles he initially shared were primarily physical and emotional, but I wondered what else might be going on. I offered to serve him as a soul friend, and he accepted. As we talked, it became clear that Mark knew a lot about God, but was uncomfortable when I talked about an interactive relationship with God. When I mentioned that prayer was about listening to God as well as talking, Mark grew suspicious. He asserted that God spoke to us through the Bible. I agreed with Him and shared with him about the life and teachings of Christ as they point us to the reality of an experiential relationship with God. This concept stretched Mark's boundaries quite a bit. I knew the feeling because I had once been in the same place as he. I too had been taught that experience was not to be trusted; and yet, I had frequently heard, "Christianity is not a religion, it's a relationship." Sounds simple enough…but what does this really mean? And how do you have a relationship without experiencing the other person?

Mark's choice to trust me was an exercise of the will. It was a choice to enter into community with me. Mark was making other good choices as well: choosing to read, pray, reflect, and follow through on our discussions. Over the next couple of months, Mark began to hope for more. He began to believe that God could still speak today – that an actual relationship with God was possible.

He began to move from the *idea* of relationship to living it out in a transformational way. As he gained a more accurate picture of God, himself, and the world around him – including *The Five Circles* – both his thinking and his feelings were changing. Hope was growing.

As Mark read the Gospels with an eye on Jesus' relationship with the Father, his prayer life began to change. He began to experience God more frequently and each new experience of God spurred him on even more. As this happened, the Spirit led Mark to reexamine some of the formative experiences and relationships in his past. He gained new insights into how some of these incidents were continuing to influence his current relationships, including his relationship with God. It wasn't an easy season, but growth rarely comes without hardship.

During this season of exciting growth, his wife's health began to deteriorate. Kelly suffered from chronic pain and fatigue, and this placed additional strain on their family. As a couple they struggled to understand the causes and searched for solutions. During this time, I encouraged them to continue to seek medical help, and not to forget the spiritual dimension as well. As they began to deal with these struggles on a spiritual level, the situation seemed to get worse. Their children had nightmares and strange things happened in their lives that discouraged them and distracted them from standing their ground against the devil and his minions.[244] Peter describes the devil as a roaring lion.[245] When we resist demons in Jesus' Name, they have to flee; and as they flee, they like to roar a bit. If we will stand firm, in the power of Christ, they have to leave.[246] Mark and Kelly were experiencing this. As they stayed the course, they found greater freedom on the other side.

While Mark and Kelly were fighting issues on a spiritual level, they continued to seek good medical care. They had tried a number of approaches, but none had produced the hoped-for healing. As they learned to fight spiritually, they found a new doctor and began a new treatment. Over the next few weeks, Kelly began feeling progressively stronger. In fact, I recently talked to her; she has begun to exercise again, something that was not possible before. Her recovery has been remarkably quick. In the process, they have experienced God in new ways as a family.

So, was the healing physical or spiritual? I don't know. I wonder if this either/or question is actually part of the problem. Perhaps it is more helpful to think of it as both/and. I know that dealing with things on a spiritual level has helped their family in many ways, even if Kelly's healing is not solely attributable to the spiritual steps they took.

We do not have to understand exactly what happened. Using *The Five Circles* helps us to address issues from different angles. We can allow the mystery to remain. The desire for scientific clarity on the process of healing is not the point. The point is that Mark and Kelly are growing in their relationship with God and they are becoming more and more who they were created to be. Their story illustrates how a multi-faceted pursuit of God can work in the real world.

God is calling you. He is inviting you to diligently seek Him. If you do, He will reward you.[247] I don't know what that will look like in your life. For some it will mean physical healing or reunited families, for others it may mean peace amidst the pain. I do know that God loves you so much that He sent His Son so that you could know Him and come to the party.[248] He has issued the invitation and made a way for you. He has done all that is necessary. You need only to respond.

Come…share in our joy.

CONCLUSION: REFLECTION QUESTIONS

- *What part(s) of Mark and Kelly's journey resonate(s) with you? Have you intentionally pursued all the areas of growth, as they have?*

- *Is there a specific area of your life where you are struggling? If so, how might you apply* The Five Circles *to address it?*

- *How can you apply* The Five Circles *to help you to grow in your relationship with God? With others? In your personal life?*

- *How will your approach to your relationship with God, the Triune Community, be informed or transformed by what you have read in this book?*

- *What is God calling you to do in response to what you have read?*

- *With whom can you share your journey and find encouragement for the road ahead?*

Bibliography

Additional information on some of these resources is listed topically in Appendix A.

Alcorn, Randy. *Heaven*. Wheaton, IL: Tyndale House, 2004.

American Time Use Survey Summary. http://www.bls.gov/news. release/atus.nr0.htm. Accessed September 2011.

Anderson, Neil T. *The Bondage Breaker*. Eugene, OR: Harvest House, 2nd edition, 2000.
— *Victory Over the Darkness: Realizing the Power of Your Identity in Christ*. Ventura, CA: Regal Books, 2000.

Arnold, Clinton E. *3 Crucial Questions about Spiritual Warfare*. Grand Rapids, MI: Baker Academic, 1997.

Benner, David G. *The Gift of Being Yourself*. Downers Grove, IL: InterVarsity Press, 2004.
— *Sacred Companions: The Gift of Spiritual Friendship and Direction*. Downers Grove, IL: InterVarsity Press, 2002.
— *Surrender to Love: Discovering the Heart of Christian Spirituality*. Downers Grove, IL: InterVarsity Press, 2003.

Bright, Bill. *7 Basic Steps to Successful Fasting & Prayer*. New Life Publications, 1995.

Bubeck, Mark I. *The Adversary: The Christian Versus Demon Activity*. Chicago: Moody Press, 1975.
— *Overcoming the Adversary: Warfare Praying Against Demon Activity*. Chicago: Moody Press, 1984.

Calhoun, Adele Ahlberg. *Spiritual Disciplines Handbook: Practices That Transform Us*. Downers Grove, IL: InterVarsity Press, 2005.

Card, Michael. *A Sacred Sorrow*. Colorado Springs: NavPress, 2005.

Chesterton, G.K. *What's Wrong with the World*.
Various editions available.
— *Orthodoxy*. Various editions available.

Christian 12 Steps to Sobriety. http://www.choosehelp.com/
christian-recovery/what-are-the-christian-12-steps-to-sobriety.
Accessed July 2012.

Cloud and Townsend. *The Mom Factor*. Grand Rapids, MI:
Zondervan, 1996.

Conversations: Vol. 9.1 Spring/Summer 2011. *Spirituality and the
Body*. Back issues can be ordered from their website: http://
conversationsjournal.com/.

Crabb, Larry. *Inside Out*. Colorado Springs: NavPress, 2007.
— *The Safest Place on Earth*. Nashville: W Publishing, 1999.

Donne, John. *Devotions Upon Emergent Occasions*.
Various editions available.

Edwards, Jonathan. *The Life and Diary of David Brainerd*.
— *A Treatise Concerning Religious Affections*.
Various editions available. Originally published 1746.

Foster, Richard J. *Celebration of Discipline: The Path to Spiritual
Growth*. 25th anniv. Ed. New York: HarperCollins, 2003.
— *Freedom of Simplicity*. New York: HarperCollins, 1989.

Henslin, Dr. Earl, *This is Your Brain on Joy*. Nashville, TN:
Thomas Nelson, 2008.

Hess, Valerie E. and Lane M. Arnold. *The Life of the Body: Physical
Well-Being and Spiritual Formation*. Downers Grove, IL:
InterVarsity Press, 2013.

Hilton Jr., Donald L. *How Pornography Drugs & Changes Your
Brain*. http://www.salvomag.com/new/articles/salvo13/13hilton.
php. Accessed September 2011.

Johnson, Dr. Darrell, *Experiencing the Trinity*. Vancouver:
Regent College Publishing, 2002.

Laubach, Frank. *Letters from a Modern Mystic.*
Various editions available.

Lewis, C.S. *The Weight of Glory.* Various editions available.

Lingenfelter, Sherwood G. *Transforming Culture: A Challenge for
Christian Mission.* Grand Rapids: Baker Books, 1998.

MacLeslie, T.J. *Pursuit of a Thirsty Fool.* Orlando:
BottomLine Media, 2011.

Moreland, J.P. *Loving God with All Your Mind: The Role of Reason in
the Life of the Soul.* Colorado Springs: NavPress, 1997.
— *Kingdom Triangle: Recover the Christian Mind, Renovate the Soul,
Restore the Spirit's Power.* Grand Rapids, MI: Zondervan, 2007.

Nouwen, Henri. *The Way of the Heart.* New York:
Ballantine Books, 1983.

Pascal, Blaise. *Pensées.* Various editions available.

Piper, John. *Desiring God.* Colorado Springs: Multnomah, 2003.

Ryan, Dale and Juanita. *A Spiritual Kindergarten: Christian
Perspectives on the Twelve Steps.* Brea, CA:
Christian Recovery International, 2008.

Ryan, Dale and Juanita and VanVonderen, Jeff. *Soul Repair:
Repairing your Spiritual Life.* Downers Grove, IL:
InterVarsity Press, 2008.

Scazzero, Peter, *Emotionally Healthy Spirituality.* Nashville, TN:
Thomas Nelson, 2006.

St. Augustine. *The Confessions of St. Augustine.*
Various editions available.

St. Patrick. *The Confession of St. Patrick.* Various editions available.

Thomas, Gary. *Sacred Pathways.* Grand Rapids: Zondervan, 2000.
Additional information including a free study guide is available
online at http://garythomas.com/books/sacred-pathways/.

Tozer, A.W. *The Knowledge of the Holy.* New York:
HarperCollins, 1961.

Tzu, Sun. *The Art of War*. Various editions available.

Willard, Dallas. *The Divine Conspiracy: Rediscovering Our Hidden Life in God*. New York: HarperCollins, 1998.

— *Hearing God*. Downers Grove, IL: InterVarsity Press, 2012.

— *New Age of Ancient Christian Spirituality*. http://www.dwillard. org/articles/artview.asp?artID=95. Accessed September 2011.

— *The Spirit of the Disciplines: Understanding How God Changes Lives*. New York: HarperCollins, 1988.

— *Renovation of the Heart: Putting On the Character of Christ*. Colorado Springs: NavPress, 2002.

Appendices

The Five Circles is an overarching paradigm. This book cannot cover any of the subjects in the depth they require. My hope is that the book has encouraged you to consider exploring new ways to grow as a person and specifically in your relationship with God. These appendices can point you in some directions that will provide help in taking the next steps of your journey.

Many of the resources are geared toward providing information about areas with which you may be unfamiliar or even uncomfortable. I hope that you will find them helpful. I also hope you will move beyond information to application. My goal is to spur you on to love and good deeds, to encourage you to make the climb, and perhaps point out some handholds that others have used on their way up.

Appendix A is a list of books and other resources that I would recommend, and a few sentences to help explain why I suggest them. They have been selected to provide information and guidance in each of *The Five Circles*. These are by no means the only books that could be helpful, just a few I would personally recommend. Not every book in the bibliography is contained here, so you may want to also see the Bibliography for additional resources.

Appendix B has several tools I find of benefit when working through *The Five Circles* myself and with others. The first is a compilation of some of the questions I find helpful when using *The Five Circles* as an assessment tool. This is followed by two tables that might be useful as alternative ways to reflect on and apply *The Five Circles*. The last tool in the section is a visual aid of the paradigm. I often use this when I am listening to a sojourner describe their situation and experience, jotting down relevant notes on the various places on the page to help me consider which area(s) might be most helpful to take next steps on their journey.

Appendix C is a list of devotional exercises broken down according to *The Five Circles*. This list is by no means exhaustive; it is intended to provide ideas and encouragement about how to take practical steps toward developing your relationship with God.

For your convenience, digital versions of all resources found in the appendices are available for download at the *Designed for Relationship* website (www.dfrbook.com). Additional resources will be added as they become available, so feel free to check back from time to time.

Additional Reading and Resources

All of the books and resources on the annotated list below are informational, and therefore all are engaging of the mind. However, I have categorized them according to *The Five Circles* in an attempt to make it easier to explore the area(s) that are of most interest to you. Some of the books could also have been otherwise categorized, so you may want to look at the whole list as you consider where to start.

THE SPIRIT

- Edwards, Jonathan. *A Treatise Concerning Religious Affections.* Various editions available. Originally published 1746.

  Although this classic may be a challenging read because of the way our language has evolved, it is well worth the effort. Edwards embraces both the emotional and intellectual aspects of our relationship with God, but centers on the spiritual change that marks all true conversion.

- Deere, Jack. *Surprised by the Voice of God.* Grand Rapids: Zondervan, 1998.

  For those (like me) who wonder how God speaks, this is an excellent place to start. Deere comes from a solidly biblical position, and encourages us to be open to hearing directly from the Spirit in a number of ways while also encouraging discernment and reaffirming biblical guidelines.

- Smith, Gordon T. *The Voice of Jesus: Discernment, Prayer, and the Witness of the Spirit.* Downers Grove, IL: InterVarsity Press, 2003.

This is another excellent book about discerning the voice of God. Perhaps a bit more scholarly than Deere's book, but another good resource for those seeking to hear from the Holy Spirit.

- Willard, Dallas. *Hearing God.* Downers Grove, IL: InterVarsity Press, 1999.

Yet another good book about how to hear and discern the voice of God. Many of Willard's books are dense and academic. I found this one more understandable and conversational. It lacks none of his careful analysis, but shares his personal journey of learning how to hear God. His work, *The Divine Conspiracy* (see the Mind resources below) could also have been placed in this section.

- Anderson, Neil T. *The Bondage Breaker.* Eugene, OR: Harvest House Publishers, 2nd edition, 2000.

Originally published in 1990, this was the first book I read on spiritual warfare. It is still the one I recommend most often. It is biblical and practical, containing a section called *Steps to Freedom in Christ* that I would recommend to everyone.

- Bubeck, Mark. *The Adversary.* Chicago, Moody Publishers, 1975.

This is another of the earliest books I read on spiritual warfare. It is slightly less practical than Anderson's book, but I still recommend it as a solidly biblical approach to the topic.

THE MIND

- Piper, John. *Desiring God*. Colorado Springs: Multnomah, 2003.

  This book was a critical one for my journey. It came at just the right time and helped me to lay a new foundation for my relationship with God – one that was thoroughly biblical, but also engaged my heart in deep ways. I highly recommend this book!

- Tozer, A.W. *The Knowledge of the Holy*. New York: HarperCollins, 1961.

  An amazing blend of head and heart, this prophetic little book paints a passionate picture of the attributes of God, and calls us to think rightly about Him and ourselves.

- Benner, David G. *The Gift of Being Yourself*. Downers Grove, IL: InterVarsity Press, 2004.

  This short book is a call to discover ourselves and to bring who we really are into relationship with God. I have placed it in this section because of the way it lays a foundation for the exploration of ourselves.

- Willard, Dallas. *The Divine Conspiracy: Rediscovering Our Hidden Life in God*. New York, HarperCollins, 1998.

  While some find Willard a tough read, I find that his books are worth the effort. Willard invites us to rediscover what God is doing in and around us. His careful examination of the Scriptures and equally careful thinking call us into an experiential relationship with God.

THE WILL

- Willard, Dallas. *The Spirit of the Disciplines: Understanding How God Changes Lives.* New York: HarperCollins, 1988.

  This book lays a solid philosophical and theological base for a right understanding and practice of the spiritual disciplines. A good foundational work on exercising the will for spiritual formation.

- Foster, Richard J. *Freedom of Simplicity.* New York: HarperCollins, 1989.

  Foster calls us to examine our lives and to choose simplicity. He does not limit his call to external simplicity, but looks at the choices we need to make both internally and in our relationship with the world around us. An easy read, but challenging in other ways.

- Thomas, Gary. *Sacred Pathways.* Grand Rapids: Zondervan, 2000.

  Thomas takes a different approach to the disciplines, looking at a sort of spiritual temperament. I use this book very frequently in working with those God brings to me. I have found it helps people to identify ways to explore their relationship with God in very personal ways, but also provides guidance in the search.

- Ryan, Dale and Juanita. *A Spiritual Kindergarten: Christian Perspectives on the Twelve Steps.* Brea, CA: Christian Recovery International, 2008.

  I discovered this book recently, after reading another book by the Ryans. (see the Bibliography) It is a short but powerful book with insightful questions that have probed my soul. Although it was birthed from within the recovery world, it is highly relevant for all Christians looking to grow.

- Calhoun, Adele Ahlberg. *Spiritual Disciplines Handbook: Practices That Transform Us.* Downers Grove, IL: InterVarsity Press, 2005.

  A friend of mine recommended this book to me recently, and I only wish I had found it earlier in my journey. It is an excellent resource book with an easy-to-follow organization and useful suggestions for many spiritual disciplines. Calhoun has really practical suggestions and tools for trying out many practices. If you are not sure how to fast, or how to pray, or what practicing solitude might look like, this is your place to start.

THE EMOTIONS

- Crabb, Larry. *Inside Out*. Colorado Springs: NavPress, 2007.

  First published in 1988, this book was a critical part of my own journey. Although it is an easy read, it was hard for me to come to grips with the concepts at the time. Now, more that 20 years later, the issues raised may not seem so revolutionary, but I still highly recommend this book to people seeking to authentically and holistically pursue God.

- Benner, David G. *Surrender to Love: Discovering the Heart of Christian Spirituality*. Downers Grove, IL: InterVarsity Press, 2003.

  In this remarkably deep and insightful book, Benner calls us to move beyond intellectual belief to emotional trust with God. This is a must-read for those who want to move toward the experience of God's unconditional love for us. I also highly recommend this book because of the practical and helpful exercises included at the end of each chapter.

- Benner, David G. *Sacred Companions: The Gift of Spiritual Friendship and Direction*. Downers Grove, IL: InterVarsity Press, 2002.

  This is an excellent introduction to the idea of spiritual direction. It is both theoretical and practical, examining the history of spiritual friendship and direction as well as drawing on his own experiences to present case studies and offer practical guidance.

This is a particularly helpful resource for mentors, pastors, life coaches, and those who care for others.

- Scazzero, Peter, *Emotionally Healthy Spirituality*. Nashville, TN: Thomas Nelson, 2006.

In this book, Scazzero openly shares his own journey from emotionally unhealthy spirituality through to a new place of intimacy with God. I found his openness refreshing and his insights transferable. He calls us to something more, and points the way.

- Freedom For the Captives Ministries, *Wholeness Prayer*.

I have personally profited from this kind of prayer ministry and use it frequently with those I care for. Aside from the fact that I have personally experienced this, I also really like it because it is freely available. Their training material is free to download at http://www. en.freemin.org/Introduction.htm. They have also posted videos of their training sessions on You Tube. (Their channel is ffcm777.) Here is the link for their training videos http://www.youtube.com/ playlist?list=UUhybZItw0uZzlwKBwjBAOKw&feature=plcp.

THE BODY

- Conversations: Vol. 9.1 Spring/Summer 2011, *Spirituality and the Body*.

This journal is an excellent introduction to the topic of spiritual formation and the body. This particular edition is entirely devoted to exploring the various issues involved.

- Henslin, Dr. Earl, *This is Your Brain on Joy*. Nashville, TN: Thomas Nelson, 2008.

This intriguing book examines the brain and how it relates to our spirituality. Dr. Henslin treats the brain as an organ in the body and, using the latest methods of brain mapping, suggests that our spirituality impacts our brain, and our brain impacts our spirituality.

It is both technical and practical. I was challenged to think more deeply about the connection between the physical, emotional, and spiritual parts of ourselves. This is probably the book that challenged and encouraged me the most to think holistically.

- Foster, Richard J. *Celebration of Discipline: The Path to Spiritual Growth*. 25th anniv. Ed. New York: HarperCollins, 2003.

This modern classic explores the spiritual disciplines in more depth and practicality than many books. It specifically examines twelve traditional spiritual disciplines and recommends them as a pathway to freedom. This could just have easily been categorized under the will, but I have placed it here because so many of these disciplines involve the body.

- Bright, Bill. *7 Basic Steps to Successful Fasting & Prayer*. New Life Publications, 1995.

This little book was a great help to me when I first began to fast. I found a number of books that discussed the theology of fasting, but few that got as practical as this one, with suggestions for how to prepare for and break a fast. It is a good place to start if you are unfamiliar with fasting.

- Hess and Lane. *The Life of the Body: Physical Well-Being and Spiritual Formation*, IVP, 2013.

I was frustrated in searching for a book specifically tackling the topics in this chapter, until a friend told me about this book. His professor, Valerie Hess was kind enough to arrange for me to receive an advance copy. For those wanting to specifically explore the intersection between our physicality and our spirituality, I recommend this book!

Assessment Questions and Tools

It is with some trepidation that I have decided to include the following assessment tools. Spiritual friendship is a three-way conversation between the soul friend, the one being cared for, and God. It is not a system to be imposed, but a conversation to be had. The most important part is not the questions but the listening. The questions are not sequential. The list below should be treated more like a menu from which you might select relevant questions for your situation. Or better yet, develop your own questions as you listen carefully and the issues emerge from the discussion.

With that as the context, I offer the following questions that I have found helpful, as I have coached others, or worked on my own journey. They are intended to give you an idea of the kind of questions that might help in self-discovery or in helping others to get a sense of where they might want to focus their attention.

Throughout this process I am not taking control; I am seeking to facilitate. I am not diagnosing those I am caring for; I am helping to facilitate a process of discovery. The center of that process is their dialogue with the Holy Spirit. I am not the expert, I am merely there to help. This is a prayerful process.

For the purpose of this list, I am assuming this is the first time I have met them as their soul friend/spiritual director, and that this is the beginning of our shared journey together. Often people will be able start by sharing what has happened *to* them rather than what is happening *in* them. That is a normal place to start. Asking informational questions can help to lay a foundation of trust before going deeper. The questions below assume that kind of process.

I often use these questions in tandem with either a blank sheet of paper on which I draw *The Five Circles* or, if I have it handy, a sheet of paper with the graphical paradigm printed on it. I find the drawing very useful in explaining the paradigm and as an assessment tool. Feel free to photocopy these resources for personal or ministry use, or download the digital versions of these tools at the *Designed for Relationship* website (www.dfrbook.com). I often make notes directly onto the drawing to help visualize what I am hearing, for myself and for the person I'm working with.

It may be helpful to point out the difference between spiritual friendship and therapy. A soul friend is not usually a therapist, and therefore, may not make psychological diagnosis. Only a qualified professional may do that. When I have come across situations where psychological (or medical) help is needed, I referred those I cared for to qualified professionals. I did not stop caring for my friends, but neither did I offer help beyond my qualifications. It is important for us to humbly offer the care we are qualified to offer, while encouraging people to seek additional care when necessary.

I find a general process we adapted from a parenting book many years ago to be helpful.[249] The following four steps are sequential. My prideful temptation is often to skip the earlier steps and jump to the latter ones; however, the last two steps are not necessarily the role of a soul friend. I include them here so you can see the progression of communication.

1. **Contain** – Listen carefully. Stay present with them. Try to be aware not just of the words but of the emotions.

2. **Validate** – Reflect back to them what you are hearing. Try to identify with their experience and let them know (as much as you can) that you hear them and understand how they feel.

3. **Context** – Try to help them place their experience in the broader context of life or their situation. This is a gentle broadening of perspective. Depending on the relationship and the specifics of the situation this step may not be at all appropriate for me as their soul friend.

4. **Correct** – If there is something wrong, something they are not understanding or doing correctly, this is where that would be pointed out. This can be a really helpful step if done appropriately, but also can be very damaging if badly done. I don't correct their emotions, but I might try to help them see how their emotions spring from a misunderstanding of the facts.

Some people find tables more helpful, so I have included two tables later in this appendix which can be used for personal reflection or application, or as a tool for conversation with someone you're caring for.

QUESTIONS FOR EVALUATION

QUESTIONS TO START THE CONVERSATION

My first goal is to build trust and to establish a warm, safe context for the conversation. I open the time in prayer and invite them to join me in praying if they wish.

- *How are you today?*

- *How are you doing?*

- *What's been happening in your life?*

- *Is there anything in particular you want to talk about (or share with me)?*

- *How is your relationship with God going?*

- *On a scale of one to ten, with one being 'virtually non-existent' and ten being 'amazing,' where would you say you are in terms of an intimate relationship with God? And why?*

- *Are you experiencing any particular struggles or feeling stuck in any way?*

QUESTIONS TO EXPLORE THE NATURE OF THE ISSUE(S) RAISED

I am assuming that by this point in the conversation they have confided in me about a struggle or an issue they are facing.

- *Tell me more about (the issue or incident)?*

- *When did this start? What else was happening in your life at that time?*

- *How long have you felt this way/been experiencing this?*

- *Have you dealt with this before?*

- *How long have you been dealing with this?*

- *When did you first feel this way? Or, When did this first start happening?*

- *How did you feel about that when it happened?*

- *How frequently does this happen?*

- *Why do you think this is happening? Why do you think this keeps happening (if it is a pattern)?*

- *When does this normally happen?*

- *How do you feel when you are doing this? (if it is a pattern or compulsion) Are you aware of anything that happens just before you feel this way?*

- *What do you think triggers this?*

- *Is there anything else that you need to tell me?*

Questions to discern where they are in the process

- *How have you tried to overcome this? How has that been working out for you?*

- *Are there things you could do that would make a difference? Perhaps something you have thought of but haven't tried?*

- *Have you tried to get help before? From whom? How did that work out?*

- *What do you hope to get out of our times together?*

- *How can I help you?*

- *Have you experienced freedom in this area in the past? Tell me about that season? If so, when did this new season of struggle start again?*

QUESTIONS ABOUT SPECIFIC CIRCLES

All through the above questions, I have been listening for clues to potential factors. I then ask questions like the ones below to explore areas that have been raised thus far in the conversation.

SPIRIT

- *Tell me about your experience of God in the midst of this.*

- *Where is God in this struggle? When this is happening?*

- *At some point in your life, have you surrendered to Christ and given Him full reign over your life?*

- *Have you tried praying and inviting God into the struggle/situation?*

- *Have you considered the implications that there is someone actively seeking to destroy you? How might that awareness influence your understanding of this situation/struggle?*

- *Are you familiar with spiritual warfare?*

- *Have you consciously resisted God in this process?*

- *Have you consciously given the Devil a foothold in your life?*

- *Would you be interested in learning more about spiritual warfare, and closing any points of access you may have opened for Satan or demons to influence you?*

MIND

- *What do you think is happening?*

- *How do you understand the various issues involved?*

- *How well do you understand what is happening to/in you?*

- *Are there any other ways of understanding the issues involved?*

- *What might this look like from another perspective?*

- *Have you considered other perspectives, perhaps the perspectives or experiences of others involved or affected by this struggle?*

- *Are you familiar with the biblical teaching on the subject?*

WILL

- *What choices have you made that have contributed to/influenced this situation/struggle?*

- *Are there different choices you could make? Perhaps choices earlier in the process? Perhaps lifestyle choices that would alleviate some of the underlying factors?*

- *Describe your lifestyle to me.*

- *What choices are you making daily/consistently that are either helping or hindering this situation?*

- *Would you describe yourself as a disciplined person?*

- *Do you do things regularly to strengthen your ability to make hard choices? Fasting? Other disciplines?*

- *What spiritual disciplines do you practice regularly? How might the presence (or absence) of these be a contributing factor?*

EMOTIONS

- *How do you feel about this situation/struggle?*

- *Tell me more about how you feel before/during/after this happens?*

- *Do you have someone else that you have talked to/are talking with this about?*

- *Have you ever sought professional counseling for this or any other issue? If so, what was that experience like? If not, why not?*

- *Do you have someone (friends/family) who are supporting you in this?*

- *Do your friends/family know about this? How have they responded? If you haven't told them, why not?*

- *Have you felt this way before? When did this feeling first start?*

- *Do you remember the first time you felt this way?*

- *How would you feel about asking God about this situation/struggle?*

- *Can we spend time praying about this together and asking God for His perspective? (This might lead into a time of wholeness prayer. See the resource section above for more on this.)*

BODY

- *When did this happen? What time of day does it usually happen? (listening for patterns related to daily cycles of food and rest)*

- *Where does it happen?*

- *How were you feeling physically before/during/after this?*

- *Does this issue seem to follow a cyclical pattern? Does it come up more often in some seasons of life than others? Happen more often when you are tired?*

- *How do you feel about your body?*

- *How have you been treating yourself (your body) lately?*

- *Have you sought medical help related to this issue? Or have you considered whether or not there might be bio-medical factors involved?*

- *Are you on any prescription medication?*

- *Do you regularly take any non-prescription medication or supplements?*

THE FIVE CIRCLES VISUAL AID

THE FIVE CIRCLES

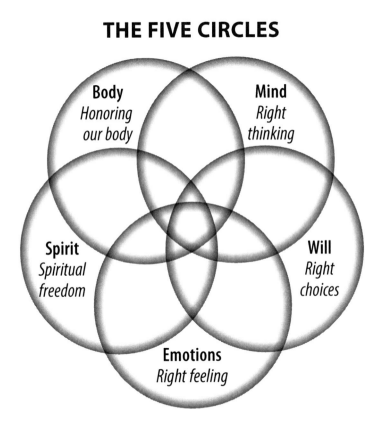

REFLECTING ON THE FIVE CIRCLES

When working through a particular issue or difficult situation, you can use this organizer to record how each applicable aspect of *The Five Circles* is playing out in your life right now (only complete the area, or areas, related to this issue). Although separated on this page for ease of use, be sure to keep in mind that each circle is integrated and overlaps with the others.

ISSUE:

SPIRIT *Spiritual Freedom*	MIND *Right Thinking*	WILL *Right Choices*	EMOTIONS *Right Feeling*	BODY *Honoring Our Body*
• Could there be a spiritual component to this issue? • How might Satan be influencing this situation?	• Are there any wrong thoughts or beliefs that have found expression in your life? • Are there other potential explanations for this situation? • What does the Bible say about this?	• What choices are you making regarding this issue? Are they hindering your relationship with God? • Are there contributing lifestyle choices you are making, or could make?	• Is your emotional development affecting this issue? • How does this issue affect your relationships? • Who can you talk to about this?	• Are you taking care of your body? • Is there a physical dimension to this issue?

APPLYING THE FIVE CIRCLES

After reflecting on *The Five Circles*, think and pray about your next steps. What are some possible avenues for resolving this issue? For each applicable area, jot down a few practical and attainable goals that can help resolve the issue.

ISSUE:

SPIRIT Spiritual Freedom	MIND Right Thinking	WILL Right Choices	EMOTIONS Right Feeling	BODY Honoring Our Body
• What are you intentionally doing to resist the Devil and his schemes? • Have you prayed about this and invited others to pray for you?	• What can you do to combat wrong thinking? • Who can you ask to provide some additional perspective on this issue, perhaps helping you to see a blind spot? • What are some practical steps you can take to grow in your knowledge of God?	• What spiritual disciplines can help you make choices that will move your relationship with God forward? • Do you need to make any lifestyle changes? • Are there bad choices you are making that you need to stop?	• What are some practical ways you can grow emotionally regarding this issue? • Who can you confide in about these issues? • How might prior emotional experiences be contributing to this issue?	• What practical steps can you take to make sure you have a healthy balance in regards to your body? • What can you do to honor God with your body? • Are there contributing medical factors? If so what, if anything, can you do to get help with those?

Devotional Exercises

There are many different paths along which we can and will encounter God. All legitimate paths will lead us toward increasing intimacy with the Triune God we find in the Bible. This diversity-loving Community of God has created us each as unique expressions of His love and image. He has placed us within unique cultural and familial settings as well. As a result, we are all very different, and while He never changes, our experiences of Him will be unique and very personal.

God will occasionally ambush us when we least expect it, but that doesn't mean that we should not actively cultivate our relationship with God. Devotional exercises are the practices that we do to intentionally develop our awareness of Him. There are many different practices available to us, and it can be hard to know where to start.

I recommend starting with Gary Thomas' *Sacred Pathways* approach to identify a few key areas that might be particularly helpful for you. There is a free study guide available from his website to help you get started today: http://garythomas.com/books/sacred-pathways/.

Once you have identified a practice you would like to try, I highly recommend Calhoun's *Spiritual Disciplines Handbook* as a fairly exhaustive and practical 'how to' manual. Calhoun breaks down the disciplines into categories and provides lots of specific ways the disciplines can be implemented. It is not a book to be read front to back, but is a great resource for how to try various disciplines.

I will resist the temptation to recommend particular practices to you, and leave you to prayerfully consider your next step. Although our devotional exercises don't neatly fall into isolated categories, I have included a table below to point you to some practices that might be helpful in growing in each of *The Five Circles*.

May God lead you to Himself as you seek Him along these, and other, paths!

SPIRIT	MIND	WILL	EMOTIONS	BODY
• Solitude • Silence • Spiritual Retreats • Sacraments • Creating Sacred Space	• Memorizing Scripture • Bible Reading Plans • Bible Study	• Prayer Cards • Voluntary vows to God • Daily Office/Hours	• Prayer of Examen • Drawing/ Art Therapy • Journaling • Listening to Music • Celebration • Corporate Worship	• Prayer Walking • Fasting • Sacraments

Notes

PREFACE

1 2 Corinthians 1:3-4
2 Hebrews 10:24

INTRODUCTION

3 John 10:10
4 Jeremiah 2:11-13; Proverbs 5
5 The book of Hosea in the Old Testament contains the story of the prophet Hosea. Hosea was called to live his life as a prophecy before the people of God. God commanded him to marry a prostitute, Gomer, who was habitually unfaithful to him. This is perhaps the most potent expression of the tragic love affair between God and man, as well as perhaps the most difficult prophetic ministry contained in the Scriptures.
6 Perhaps the clearest Scripture on this is found in Revelation 3:20 where Jesus describes Himself as standing at the door and knocking. He promises that if we will hear and open the door that He will come in and sit down to a meal with us. It is such a tangible and personal expression of the relational heart of God. It is also telling that this message was given to the church. It is not just people outside of the church who need to hear His knock and respond to His invitation to real relationship.
7 By saint here, I mean a rarefied picture of holiness. Of course, every follower of Christ is a saint, one set apart for God, in the general sense.
8 C.S. Lewis , 'The Weight of Glory'. *The Weight of Glory and Other Addresses*. New York: Simon and Schuster, 1996.

CHAPTER 1

9 The original story is found in Luke 15:11-32.
10 Luke 15:29
11 James 4:2b-
12 Genesis 1:26. Scholars continue to debate the complexities of Hebrew grammar and we should not base our entire understanding of the Trinity on this passage alone; however, this passage in the opening pages of Scripture introduces the possibility

of the community of God. The Trinity is hinted at in many passages in the Old Testament, particularly the prophets, but is more explicitly explained in the New Testament. A few key New Testament passages to consider are: Matthew 28:19; Mark 1:9-11; John 1:1; 14:1-17, 16:1-15 and 17:1-26; 2 Corinthians 13:14; Ephesians 1:2-14; 2 Thessalonians 2:13-14; and 1 Peter 1:2.

13   I am not alone in struggling with language to express this mystery. While the reality of the Trinity is clearly found throughout Scripture, the early church councils worked hard to formulate language that would clarify the Trinity and provide unity for the church, capturing and expressing our beliefs in the early creeds of Christendom. The Nicean and Athanasian creeds particularly struggle to describe/define the Trinity.

14   Genesis 1-2
15   Revelation 22:7, 12
16   Revelation 22:17
17   Revelation 22:17
18   John 7:37-39
19   John 5:39-40
20   John 10:10
21   John 14:12
22   John 17:3
23   John 14:6
24   Luke 11:11-13
25   Psalm 84:11; Matthew 7:11

CHAPTER 2

26   Genesis 3; Romans 5:12
27   Romans 1:19-20; Psalm 19:1
28   John 1:14
29   Philippians 2: 5-11
30   1 Peter 1:3-5 and 2 Peter 1:3-4
31   The story of how I ended up here is told in *Pursuit of a Thirsty Fool.*
32   Matthew 23 contains some of Jesus' harshest rebukes and it is for the religious people of His day who knew the truth, but failed to practice it. In doing so, they prevented others from coming into the Kingdom of Heaven.
33   *What's Wrong With The World, Part One: The Homelessness Of Man*, Ch. 5: The Unfinished Temple.
34   Hebrews 11:6
35   In Buddhism, there is no God. The only hope is to escape from desire. The only hope is to kill your hope. The only hope is to stop wanting something more and to achieve nothingness. To become nothing is the great release.
     In Hinduism, the world is an illusion and the only hope is escape. There are thousands of gods, but still no hope. There is no intimacy with God or the gods. They are capricious and territorial. These gods are like the gods of the Greeks and Romans, to be feared and placated, but not to be loved. The only hope is to escape from the cycle of life. Again, nothingness is the only hope.
     In Islam, there is One God, but He is fierce, holy, and completely other, unknowable. The only choice for the believer is submission to His law and a plea for mercy. Even in heaven, there is no promise of intimacy or relationship with God, but rather a promise of satisfaction of sensual desires.
     Perhaps more insidious than these is the lie that God does not exist or at the least

is unknowable. This lie puffs us up and tears us down at the same time. It tells us that we are the pinnacle of the world and that God is either watching us from a distance like a watchmaker, dispassionately watching the mainspring of His creation wind down, or simply a figment of our imagination or a delusional product of our biochemistry. This leaves us free from moral restraint but also debases us and frees us to use and debase others as merely objects in the universe. The lie of secular humanism is rapidly capturing the minds of many.

36 Isaiah 53:4-6
37 1 John 4:9-10; Romans 5:8-10; and John 1:9-10, 14
38 Revelation 21:5
39 Matthew 24:14
40 Psalm 34:8
41 Exodus 20:18-19
42 Romans 1:20
43 The Confession of St. Patrick; The Confessions of St. Augustine; The Life and Diary of David Brainerd by Jonathan Edwards; Letters from a Modern Mystic by Frank Laubach.

CHAPTER 3
44 John 4
45 2 Tim 3: 5
46 Romans 1:21-23
47 John 5:39-40
48 Luke 11:11-13; Romans 8:15-17; 1 John 3:1
49 John 15:15
50 Romans 8:29; Matthew 12:48-50
51 John 10:27
52 Ephesians 3:16-19
53 2 Peter 1:3-4

CHAPTER 4
54 Matthew 22:36-40
55 Sherwood Lingenfelter – *Transforming Culture*. Lingenfelter also points out that cultures are 'palaces' because they offer benefits as well. Cultures are mixed at best, shaping our worldview in ways that warp our perspective while simultaneously providing enough community to sustain life.
56 Psalm 139:1-16
57 Romans 8:14-15; Galatians 4:3-6
58 Genesis 2:18
59 John Donne Devotions upon emergent occasions - *Meditation XVII*, 1624.
60 Titus 2
61 *The Mom Factor* by Cloud and Townsend deals with this topic extensively.
62 Even the pastoral epistles, written to individuals, were primarily concerned about the communities these individuals were leading. The only other book written to an individual is Philemon which was about the restoration of relationship between two estranged Christian brothers.
63 Hebrews 10:24-25
64 John 13:34
65 *Restoring the Woven Cord: Strands of Celtic Christianity for the Church Today* by Michael Mitton, BRF (The Bible Reading Fellowship); 2nd Revised edition (2010) particularly chapter 6.

66 David Benner's book, *Sacred Companions*, is probably the best introduction
to this concept.
67 John 17:20-23
68 John 14:12-15
69 Galatians 5:1; John 8:31-32
70 Matthew 6:10
71 Philippians 3:14
72 Matthew 28:20

CHAPTER 5
73 Mark 12:30
74 Matthew 22:37-38
75 Mark 12:30
76 Deuteronomy 6:5
77 John 10:10 and 14:12
78 Matthew 10:30
79 Psalm 139
80 Ephesians 4:1-16; 2 Corinthians 10:12-18; Romans 11:33-12:3
81 Ephesians 2:10
82 John 15:5-17
83 2 Peter 1:3
84 2 Corinthians 3:18
85 1 Peter 2:9-10
86 Romans 8:11; Galatians 5:1
87 Ephesians 2:8-10,2 Corinthians 10:3-5
88 John 8:36; Galatians 5:1
89 Matthew 23:27-28 and 5:27-28
90 The traditional theological term for this is 'progressive sanctification.' Essentially, we
become more and more like Christ in our attitudes as well as our behavior. What I am
proposing is that we renew our vision of what is possible and set our sights on true
Christlike character and experience. We will live and experience life more and more
as Christ did as we become more and more transformed from the inside out into His
image. As the image of God is restored in us, we will attain the freedom that He had.
91 Romans 8:28-39
92 Ephesians 5:18; Galatians 5:16-17
93 John 10:10
94 Matthew 4:1-11 (parallel passages in Mark 1 and Luke 4).
95 Jeremiah 2:11-13; John 7:37-38
96 Those familiar with the 12 steps will recognize I am paraphrasing step 2 here. The
12 steps originated in Alcoholics Anonymous; but have been paraphrased and used
widely in recovery movements beyond alcoholism. I prefer the explicitly Christian
version of the 12 steps over the generic version. An example of the Christian version
can be found here: http://www.choosehelp.com/christian-recovery/what-are-the-
christian-12-steps-to-sobriety. I also highly recommend *A Spiritual Kindergarten:
Christian Perspectives on the Twelve Steps* by Dale and Juanita Ryan. This brief but
excellent book explains the 12 steps as one way of understanding and applying the
Gospel to our everyday lives as Christians.
97 John 10:27
98 Acts 17:10-11

99   John 8:32
100 A friend pointed out that some of the language in this second rendering of the model uses some terms that are similar to the *Noble Eightfold Path of Buddhism.* This is entirely coincidental. The content of *The Five Circles* bears no resemblance to the *Eightfold Path* beyond a few regrettable similarities in terminology.
101 2 Corinthians 3:18
102 I suggest David Benner's book, *The Gift of Being Yourself,* to read more on this idea.
103 Matthew 22:37-38; Romans 12:1-2; Ephesians 4:1-3

CHAPTER 6
104 1 Corinthians 12:12-31
105 I have dealt with this story at length in *Pursuit of a Thirsty Fool* and so I'm quickly summarizing here.
106 Mark 7:23
107 Neil Anderson, *The Bondage Breaker* and *Victory Over the Darkness.* Also Mark Bubeck, *The Adversary and Overcoming the Adversary.*
108 This was dramatically demonstrated later in my life through the miraculous healing of my wife. There is more on this story in *Pursuit of a Thirsty Fool.*
109 Jeremiah 2:11-13
110 Philippians 3:12-14

CHAPTER 7
111 John 4: 24
112 When I use the word conversion, I am not talking about abandoning one set of intellectual beliefs for another, or exchanging one ethnic identity for another. I am talking about spiritual change that takes place within us.
113 Ephesians 2:1-10; Matthew 22:1-14
114 All the names in the case studies have been changed as well as other potentially identifying details.
115 This account was originally published in *Pursuit of a Thirsty Fool*, Chapter 11.
116 Genesis 2:17; Romans 5:12-6:23; Ephesians 2:1-10
117 2 Corinthians 5:17; Revelation 21:5
118 Ephesians 2:8-10
119 2 Corinthians 1:22 and 5:5; Romans 8:23; John 7:37-38
120 I am indebted to Dallas Willard's thoughts on the subject which, although they are not the main point of this article, are summarized in the middle of the article. http://www.dwillard.org/articles/artview.asp?artID=95
121 John 3:1-21
122 Philippians 2:12
123 Mark 3:14-15
124 Romans 1:21-23
125 Ephesians 2:1-3
126 Romans 8:2
127 Colossians 2:15
128 Ephesians 6:12
129 1 Peter 5:8
130 John 8:44
131 Sun Tzu, *The Art of War* Chapter 1 paragraph 18.
132 Mark 9:29
133 1 Peter 5:8

134 Ephesians 6:10-18
135 Ephesians 6:10-18
136 I have several book recommendations on this topic in the bibliography, but the one I use most often is Neil T. Anderson's, *The Bondage Breaker*.
137 2 Corinthians 5:20. Neil Anderson's book, *Victory Over the Darkness* is an excellent resource in this area.
138 1 John 4:4; Romans 8:31
139 Matthew 16:18
140 Ephesians 6:10-20
141 James 4:7
142 1 Peter 5:8; Ephesians 6; 2 Corinthians 2
143 Ephesians 2:1-5
144 Hebrews 7:25
145 Ephesians 4:27
146 Jesus is not afraid to point this out to His opponents, nor His followers, when they act this way. John 8:44; Luke 4:8; Matthew 16:23
147 Ephesians 4:27; Matthew 12:43-45
148 Revelation 3:20
149 1 Peter 5:8-9; Galatians 5:25

CHAPTER 8
150 Ephesians 5:3
151 Ephesians 5:18
152 A. W. Tozer, *The Knowledge of the Holy* p. 1.
153 *Pragmatism and American Culture*, Gail Kennedy, Boston: Heath, 1950.
154 *Pragmatism*, William James, 1907.
155 Romans 1:18-25 speaks to the fact that no man has an excuse, because there are things we can learn about God from the world He created; however, Romans 10:14-15 points out the necessity of telling others about Christ, as the specifics of the salvation story cannot be known unless someone presents it.
156 Some may point out that God is not limited by man as a messenger. While I have no wish to limit God, He certainly does work in mysterious ways; I think it is safe to say that He generally spreads the message from person to person. The importance of being message-bearers is clear throughout Scripture.
157 Matthew 28:18-20
158 Matthew 5:17
159 2 Timothy 2:15
160 James 3:1
161 Acts 20:29, Galatians 4:17; 2 Peter 2; 2 John 7-10
162 Matthew 4:1-11
163 *Name That Tune* was an American television show where the contestants would bid against one another in an attempt to see who could recognize a popular piece of music from the fewest musical notes of the melody.
164 Romans 1:18-20; Psalm 19
165 John 16:13
166 2 Timothy 3:16; Psalm 19
167 An interesting side note (interesting to me at least): While I was writing this book, scientists claimed to have discovered subatomic particles travelling faster than the speed of light. This discovery, which made headlines around the world, calls into

question scientific tenets of belief that have been held as law. Headlines called into question Einstein's explanation of the universe, which underpins much of modern scientific thought, because of this new data. A few months later, the earth-shattering discovery turned out to be due to some badly-calibrated equipment. Apparently, Einstein's theories continue to hold…for the moment. We must hold all our interpretations in science and theology somewhat tentatively, with all humility.

168 At the same time, simply claiming belief in the Bible is not an end-all defense for holding any doctrinal position. Sincere Bible belief is not license to do anything you want with the Scriptures.

169 Proverbs 27:17; Titus 3:2

170 A common formulation for unity among Christians that is frequently (but falsely) attributed to St. Augustine.

171 John 14:9; Colossians 1:15

172 Hebrews 4:15

173 James 4:8

174 Matthew 7:8

CHAPTER 9

175 Hebrews 10:24

176 Galatians 6:7

177 Galatians 5:22-23

178 Revelation 1:8, 21:6 and 22:13

179 Colossians 1:17

180 Psalm 139:16

181 This is not a book about pre-destination and free will. I am not going to spend a lot of time taking specific theological positions on a topic like this. Instead, I will try to stick to the clearer passages and ideas, and allow the reader to continue to wrestle with the more mysterious ideas. I am not seeking to resolve every tension, but rather to appeal to the broad agreement across camps. I remember this maxim from seminary: It is not my job to explain why the Bible says something, only to show you that it says it. I believe it is a paraphrase of B.B. Warfield.

182 Genesis 3:6

183 Psalm 119:105

184 Pascal did not believe the odds were even for or against God, but rather that there are some things that we cannot solve with reason alone – we need experience. He also pointed out that if we wager on God, we have everything to gain and nothing to lose, which makes it the only reasonable bet to place.

185 Blaise Pascal, *Pensées*, Part III, Section 233.

186 Pascal says that it is a wager in the hope that it might be true, rather than an act of faith. Faith cannot be transmitted from one person to another. Faith grows through experience. And this experience is found on the road of pursuit.

187 Jeremiah 2:13

188 Thomas, Gary. *Sacred Pathways*. Grand Rapids: Zondervan, 2000.

189 Nouwen, Henri. *The Way of the Heart*. New York: Ballantine Books, 1983.

190 Hebrews 10:25

191 Psalm 23:3

192 Michael Card, *Sacred Sorrow*, Chapter 8.

193 Job 42:7

194 Job 42:7-10

195 Genesis 32:24-32
196 Romans 11
197 2 Corinthians 4:16; Romans 12:2
198 Romans 12:1

CHAPTER 10

199 Psalm 118:8; Proverbs 3:5-6 and 29:25; Isaiah 26:4
200 Just a few verses referencing God's emotions: Genesis 6:6-7; Deuteronomy 1:37, 7:8, 12:31 and 32:19; Psalms 11:5 and 78:40; Isaiah 62:5 and 63:10; Hosea 14:4; Amos 5:21; Zephaniah 3:17; Malachi 2:16; Mark 3:5 and 10:21; Luke 10:21; John 11:35 and 15:11; Ephesians 4:30 and 5:2; 1 John 4:7-21
201 A. W. Tozer, *The Knowledge of the Holy*, p. 2.
202 Proverbs 4:13
203 Matthew 15:10-20; Mark 7:14-23
204 Matthew 22:37-8
205 Hebrews 13:14
206 1 John 4:18. I am deeply indebted to David Benner's book, *Surrender to Love*, for some of these insights.
207 Isaiah 53:3; Mark 10:33-34; John 1:10-11
208 1 John 4:20
209 2 Corinthians 1:4
210 I believe that this understanding is consistent with Christ's teaching on divine and human forgiveness in Matthew 6:14-15 and 18:35.
211 John 7:37-38
212 Malachi 4:2
213 Larry Crabb has written extensively on this including, *Inside Out, The Safest Place on Earth*, and other books.
214 The particular model I employed with Sam is called wholeness prayer. More information about this model and training resources can be found in the Resources section at the end of this book.
215 Some would also place Theophostic prayer ministry into this category. http://www. theophostic.com/page12414933.aspx
216 As one learns how to use these methods, it can be done alone, but it is often helpful to have someone else involved when learning.
217 Matthew 22:37
218 Isaiah 53:6
219 Ephesians 3:11-12; Hebrews 4:14-16
220 Galatians 5:25

CHAPTER 11

221 An interesting journal devoted to this issue just came out: The *Conversations Journal* Spring/Summer 2011 edition. http://conversationsjournal.com/
222 This is an excellent article on addiction and its affect on the brain. http://www. salvomag.com/new/articles/salvo13/13hilton.php (accessed 9/1/2011)
223 *This is Your Brain on Joy* by Dr. Earl Henslin is an excellent and practical book explaining the science in relatively easy to understand terms and giving suggestions to help re-wire the brain. He has worked closely with Dr. Daniel G Amen, the famous brain scan researcher and clinician.
224 In every era, we can find extreme ascetics who attack their bodies as if they are the problem. We can also find others who indulge sensual pleasure or invest heavily in

their pursuit of their own idea of physical perfection. It is interesting that at both extremes are people who cut the body and draw blood in their pursuit. Whether it is the whip of the self-flagellant, or the scalpel of the plastic surgeon, both speak to an unhealthy over-emphasis on the body. *The Life of the Body* by Hess and Arnold deals with various approaches to the body in history and culture.

225 1 Corinthians 3:16 and 6:19
226 Genesis 2:7
227 Genesis 1:31
228 Genesis 2:15-3:7
229 1 Corinthians 6:19
230 Romans 6:13 and 12:1
231 1 Corinthians 15:12-23; 2 Corinthians 5:1-10
232 Randy Alcorn's book, *Heaven*, is an outstanding examination of the topic of heaven. He examines the Bible and paints a compelling picture of what we can expect; it is very physical. This may be surprising to some because of common cultural misconceptions about heaven, but it is clearly biblical.
233 *American Time Use Survey Summary*. http://www.bls.gov/news.release/atus.nr0.htm (accessed 9/1/2011)
234 1 Corinthians 9:26-27
235 1 Corinthians 6:19-20
236 1 Corinthians 9
237 1 Timothy 4:8
238 http://www.ihrsa.org/media-center/2011/4/5/us-health-club-membership-exceeds-50-million-up-108-industry.html (accessed 9/1/2011)
239 *American Time Use Survey Summary*; see note 233 above.
240 God even used suffering in Jesus life. Hebrews 2:10
241 1 Corinthians 10:31

CONCLUSION
242 Genesis 2
243 Matthew 22:37-38
244 Ephesians 6
245 1 Peter 5:8
246 James 4:7
247 Hebrews 11:6
248 John 3:16

APPENDIX B
249 These four steps are adapted from *The Jewels* found in chapter 5 of *The Mom Factor* by Cloud and Townsend.

CPSIA information can be obtained at www.ICGtesting.com
Printed in the USA
BVOW06*0312071013

332543BV00001B/2/P